ENGLISH-MAN

BEGGAR-MAN

HOLY-MAN

Teenage "Hippy" becomes a Sadhu, (Holy-man), and Yogi in India

RAYMOND PATTISON

(Ex-monk Paramhansa Ganesh Giri)

Copyright © 2012 Author *Raymond Pattison*

All rights reserved.

ISBN: 978-0-473-64746-9

CONTENTS

Introduction

Chapter 1. To Istanbul   Pg.5

Chapter 2. A long way from home   Pg.11

Chapter 3. Last years as an Englishman   Pg.40

Chapter 4. Holy Land   Pg.67

Chapter 5. Guru Found   Pg. 85

Chapter 6. A Guru Lost   Pg. 108

Chapter 7. A Sadhu's Life   Pg. 128

Chapter 8. The Ochre Robes   Pg. 152

Chapter 9. More Holy Men   Pg. 177

Chapter 10. The Sat Guru   Pg. 200

Chapter 11. New Home   Pg. 221

Chapter 12. Goodbye India   Pg. 252

I wrote this book in the mid 80's.

The book covers a period from 1965 to 1976.

My other books add my spiritual "teachings" & some delve into the following years, including my time as a mental health professional.

There are Sanskrit words, in *italics* for first use except person and place names. Italics also used on other occasions for emphasis. (Including Sanskrit words).

Introduction

English-Man, Beggar-Man, Holy-Man

In 1965 I left England and I spent a year travelling overland until I reached India. I only planned to go as far as Istanbul. However I found myself on what became known as the "hippy trail".

I was 17 when I left home and 18 when I reached India.

By the time I got to India I was physically and mentally exhausted. Looking back I was probably clinically depressed, physically unwell, and suffering from the effects of too much cannabis use.

I found myself in a spiritual centre called an *ashram*.

I met my first *Guru*, (my spiritual teacher) – a *Swami* & *sannyasin* renunciate in ochre robes.

I never had at that time any intention of becoming a monk for 10 years.

However I spent 10 years in India living the life of a monk otherwise known as a sadhu, who sometimes travelled and eventually saw nearly every part of India.

The first few chapters of my book talks about my travel through various countries of Europe and Asia, in the days before the name "hippy" or "flower power people" was known (I was a "beatnik).

I then talk about my time with my first Guru, when I became initiated into monastic Hinduism and the life of a celibate *Brahmachari*, dressed in white cloth.
I was that teacher's disciple for over four years.
He was an orthodox Swami, very high up in the hierarchy of the system, & I travelled widely with him on the religious lecture circuit.
I learnt a lot and I changed into somebody completely different from who I had been!
My book then moves on to my travels around India and my adopting of the red robes of a sannyasin, living the mendicant *sadhu* life.
I then found a new teacher in the form of Swami Muktananda who became well-known in the West.
He attracted hundreds if not thousands of Western devotees.
In the 70s there were quite a few similar teachers who became popular in the West.
It was the time of the Beatles meeting the Maharishi, (Mahesh Yogi), the "stardom" of a variety of Gurus, and interest in the spiritual practices of the East.
The book includes descriptions about *Yoga practices*, Hindu spiritual practices, and temple worship.

Also covered is the quest for Enlightenment, and descriptions of the way of life of Hindu monks & sages.

During my travels through India I describe meetings with a number of amazing & fascinating holy men and women.

I met with some well-known teachers or their disciples who became well known in the West, including Swami Prabhupada, the founder of Krishna Consciousness and Rajanish, (Osho), who became well-known in the press for his followers activities in America. (And for his eighty white Rolls Royce's).

There are descriptions of my own spiritual practice, & life in remote outposts of India.

Eventually I ceased to belong to any guru or path specifically, although I designed my own practice based on my several Gurus' teachings, plus using elements from existing religious and spiritual systems and structures.

I give information about the *Siddha,* (Perfected) Path and the role of *Shakti*, (the Goddess energy).

Further writings describe my life after departure from India, return to the West, and living a "regular" family life with a career. (From 1976 to the present 2022).

Other writings cover the themes of Goddess worship, *Kundalini* energy, *Tantric* spirituality, and the seekers path to *Siddhi*, or perfected practice, (& enlightenment).

I connect with the Western or medical views on mental health. (Particularly Depression & Addictions), & the connection or dis-connection with spiritual awareness & endeavour.

All content is also a "teaching" as it is the foundation for a specific pathway of a spiritual practice, which has been in regular use for millennia.

This pathway was established within the broad umbrella of Hinduism, and that is the foundation place in broad historical terms. (Including my own small contribution in India).

However the teaching illustrates how parts of this "religion" moved out of India in the 70,s, became popular, and gained a very large following in the West, with the advent of the gurus, (from India).

The religious dimension then became "translated" or Westernised into various practices of yoga, including not only the physical, but also encompassing other topics such as *chakras*, meditation, kundalini. (Plus the philosophical aspects).

The intention as never to compete with other religious or spiritual pathways, only to point out that the core practice illustrated originates way back in *Vedic* times, and maybe not only in India, and maybe even pre what is currently known as Hinduism.

The main issue at stake is Reality, Truth, and Unity. This issue is universal, global, and international, and cuts across religion, culture, language and belief systems. It is an issue for all seekers of Enlightenment of Realization. (*Nirvana and Moksha*).

Thus a non-religious foray into yoga practices of kundalini, chakras, and mantras, can be applied without recourse to the "old religious history", set in molding documents buried in caves!

This can be as "atheistic" or "scientific" as you want to make it! Because Truth, Consciousness, Bliss, (*Sat Chit Ananda*), has no boundaries or human rules or codes.

There are no issues with any code of conduct, moral persuasions, or societal propriety, as those domains are just personal choice, (alongside religious beliefs or even political beliefs). In our democracy we are free to think and believe, whatever we choose. Hopefully for a while!

P.S. There are some hand written sketches drawn many years ago. Added for historical flavor!

English Man, Beggar Man, Holy Man.   Raymond Pattison

CHAPTER ONE
To Istanbul

A small suburban jail in Lahore was my destination that humid morning. My companions and I entered through a brick archway gate, which led into an enclosure. The guard on the gate seemed friendly and smiled as we wandered into the compound, which was circled by a number of locked cells.

One of my newly found Swedish friends produced their cell key and ushered me into their large, dark cavern, where we then sat to await the midday meal. The cell would probably have held a dozen or more ordinary local prisoners, but now my two acquaintances had the exclusive use of the place. Their paths and. mine had crossed earlier that day in a nearby bazaar,

I had spent the previous hot and sticky night sleeping out of doors on the (grass of a Lahore park. Lahore in Pakistan is a few miles from India and the border, which at that moment was closed to land traffic following the India and Pakistan war of summer 1966. I was on route to India but could go no further as I did not have the price of a plane or boat ticket from Pakistan. My overland travels since November 1965 had brought me through Turkey and Iran, with a side trip through Syria and Jordan to Israel. That morning in Lahore I had been thinking more of my short-term food problem than of the situation of where I was to go next. I had been without money in my pocket for longer than I could remember, but up until then had always been fairly free from hunger. By that morning thought I had not eaten substantially for a day or two.

As I was walking through the bazaar, I came up behind two young Europeans with long hair. I approached them and immediately we started chatting about our travels and ourselves. They invited me to join them for some tea at a nearby cafe. Over cups of sickly-sweet tea they told me that they were Swedish and were returning home overland after a sojourn in the hippy center of Katmandu, Nepal. They too had been blocked by the closed border crossing, but they had swum across a river to enter Pakistan illegally. They had been caught, arrested, and sent to a Lahore jail. About the same time, some "hippy types" had been recently shot at doing the same crossing, and they informed me that while the Pakistan government want to put a stop to this behavior, (and had thus put them in jail for three months detention). They were still officially prisoners housed in a small local jail, but they had been given freedom to wander the streets during the day. They had also become friendly with the jail governor and had been guests at his house for several meals. They invited me back to their "home" for a meal of their prison food, which they found unpalatable and generally tipped down the toilet.

Although they were virtually penniless travelers, their detention had enabled their access to some government funds, (both Swedish and Pakistani), and they usually dined well in bazaar cafes. However bad the prison food was to the Swedes, I ate to my fill the meal of unleavened bread and watery curry, and that evening, when I returned to chat with my friends, they fed me once more.

Later, after letting myself out of the jail, I strolled back to my park for the night thinking over what the two Swedes had told me about the delights of Afghanistan. I resolved then to abandon my attempt to reach India and instead to return overland to England, passing by way of Afghanistan. I did not know then that I was not to reach England for another ten years.

I had set out from England in 1965 with only fifteen pounds in my pocket and my inexperience showed in the choice of my departure date. The day I set out, in late November 1965 was exceedingly cold, and there was snow on the ground. I carried a large hold-all containing a sleeping bag and change of clothes, and wore a heavy, warm overcoat for which I was to feel thankful in the days to come. I took all day to hitch-hike from London to Dover, where I boarded the ferry for Ostend. I arrived there late that evening, and wandered the streets in the drizzle for a while, until a man who spoke English directed me towards a cheap guest house which catered for the fishermen of Ostend. There were four or five beds to a room, slept in permanently by alternating shifts of workers.

I felt very sorry for myself with such a poor and cold start. In my naivety, I had not planned any of the details of the journey, except for my route to my destination, which was Istanbul. I had not given much thought to where I would sleep and eat, or to how I would communicate in strange countries. I could not afford to stay in guesthouses and planned therefore to sleep in the open until I reached Istanbul, where I knew accommodation was really cheap.

The next few days and nights were a shock to my system because the weather was so cold. Near Munich, where it was -10ºC, I passed the night huddled in a pedestrian subway under a main road. I could not get any sleep and began to hallucinate due to my weariness and coldness. Next morning, at first light, I was standing by the autobahn waiting for a lift, when a police car pulled up. When the solitary policeman inside the car found out that I was English, he told me in my own language to get into the car. He took me to a, police post nearby, which had a room full of televisions monitoring a stretch of the autobahn. I had been spotted on their surveillance screens and the policeman had come to investigate.

He was a very friendly chap and proceeded to give me hot coffee and rolls, whilst remarking that I must have been freezing. He explained to me that he liked the British because he fought them in World War Two: The only other police that came up to me on the autobahn were unfriendly, and told me I was hitch-hiking illegally. They rubbed their fingers together as if to say that if I had paid some money, it would have been all right to stay where I was. When I told them that I had no cash, they just drove off.

I managed to make good time with lifts through Germany and arrived in Salzburg, Austria, for my third night outdoors, this time in the snow. I walked out of Salzburg on the route south and put my sleeping bag down under the stars, on the snow. Surprisingly, I found the temperature to be warm and mild after Munich, and I slept comfortably. Another night was spent in mid - Austria, sleeping in a shed on planks of wood. It was near a village where I had found only a baker's shop open. This shop had no bread, only some very expensive fancy cake, which I bought because I was so hungry. I could not afford to eat in restaurants or cafes, not at least until Istanbul, and my diet became mainly bread with a bit of cheese. I did not much like going into the shops, partly on account of the language problem, and partly because I was aware of how shabby I looked.

I could not wash my clothes or bathe much in the early days of my travels. I did not really have much idea even of how to wash my things, because at home all such matters had been taken care of by my mother. I had almost no domestic skills, although as I traveled, I quickly learnt to take care of myself in a basic fashion.

I got a lift through Yugoslavia in a car with a man who told me he was a Greek doctor. He drove for two days, with only a short stop for sleep in the car. He did try to book me into an expensive looking hotel in Belgrade, but took me back into the car when he finally realized that I could not afford to stay in hotels. I tried to explain, but it just seemed incredible to him that an English person should be traveling in such a poor fashion.

As we motored down the center of Yugoslavia, avoiding the bullock carts that frequented this highway, the Greek stopped quite a few times to pick up local farmers. These passengers paid for their journey, and when the Greek suggested that I part with some of my meager reserve of money, I asked to be let out of the car. After I had explained by the side of the road that I needed to get free lifts as my money was for food, I was ushered back into the car. I then continued my ride to where the highway divided for Greece or Bulgaria. Up until then I had met no other hitch - hikers, although in summer there would have been a few. Some years later, the roads to Greece and beyond swarmed with young hitch - hikers with little or no money in their pockets.

I walked away in the direction of Bulgaria, as the Greek and his car zoomed off to the south. I found a small cafe and wandered in for a coffee. There I met a friendly Turk who offered to give me a lift if he passed me on the road the following day. He also changed some of my money at what he said were good rates. I missed the lift that he offered because next morning, whilst I was squatting behind some bushes, his Volkswagen raced by. I had spent the night near the Bulgarian border in a derelict farm building, having had a long lift after I left the cafe. I was probably lucky to miss the lift in the Turk's car, as I found out later that I had been given a dreadful exchange rate for my money. Who knows what other treachery he had up his sleeve?

A short walk brought me to the Bulgarian border where, although 'the guards did not seem pleased to see me, I was issued a visa. In the nineteen sixties, the holder of a British passport could wander about and live in many different countries without too many restrictions. Now in E.E.C. countries one can pass more easily without visas and entry stamps, but generally there are more restrictions if one wishes to live or work in many other lands.(Such as India).

At the Bulgarian border, the guards made me sit in a small room with windows overlooking the road. After a while an old bus pulled up, which was empty apart from a couple of people in front. The guards started to argue with the driver and pointed from time to time in my direction. Eventually the guards motioned me outside and into the bus, where two Turkish men stared in a none too friendly fashion. I remained on this bus right through Bulgaria into Turkey, and on into Istanbul. Surprising in view of the fact that the drivers remained somewhat aloof from me, and could have thrown me off any time after inheriting me from the border guards. I did find out that the men had bought the decrepit vehicle in Germany, and were intending to press it into passenger service on its arrival in Istanbul.

We trundled over the pot-holed Bulgarian roads, through a mist of snow and sleet, passing only the occasional gray-painted truck. We stopped just briefly for a quick meal in a roadside cafe, where I was given some food by the drivers. This was my last food for over twenty-four hours, as the bus did not stop at any other shops or cafes, and the drivers did not offer me any of the snacks they had in the bus. I did not mind the pangs of hunger too much, because I was glad to be out of the dismal weather in Bulgaria and then into the sunshine that I found in Turkey. Also, I had reached my destination, for the time being.

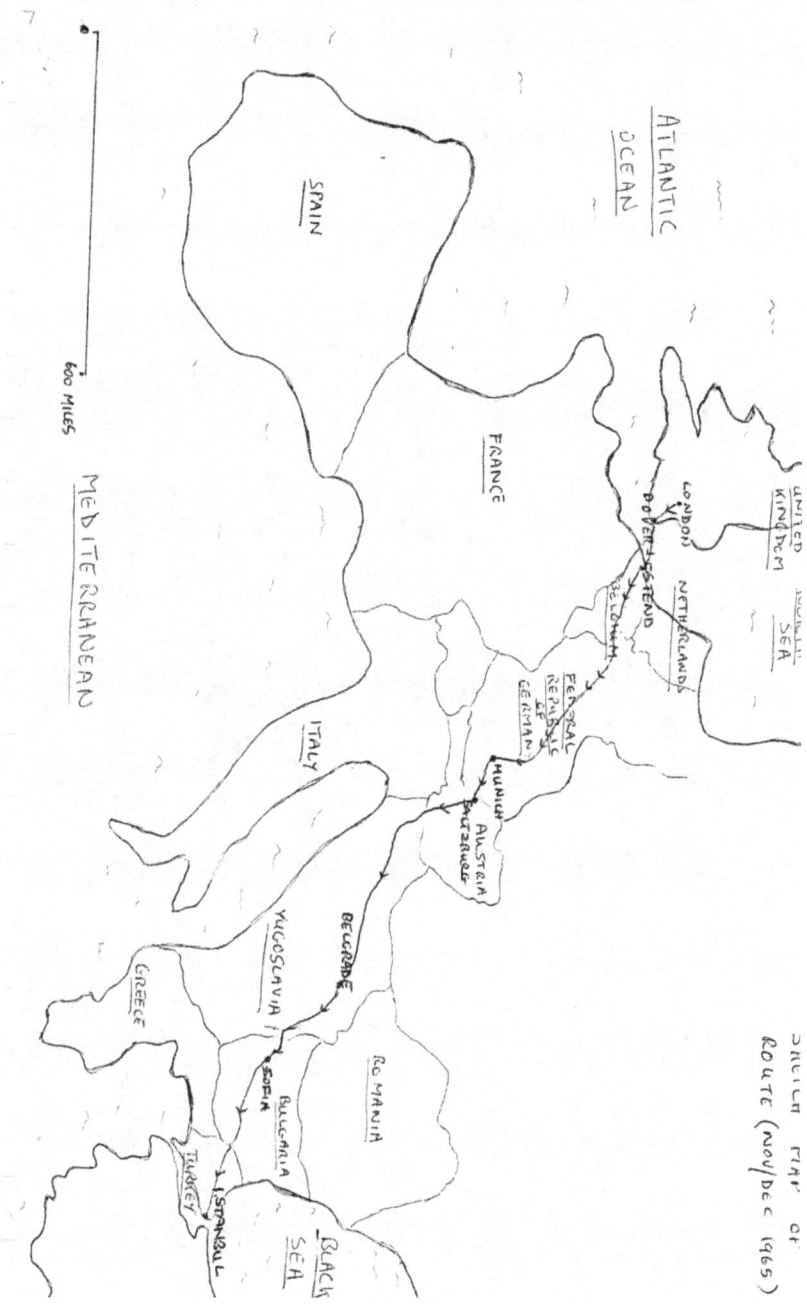

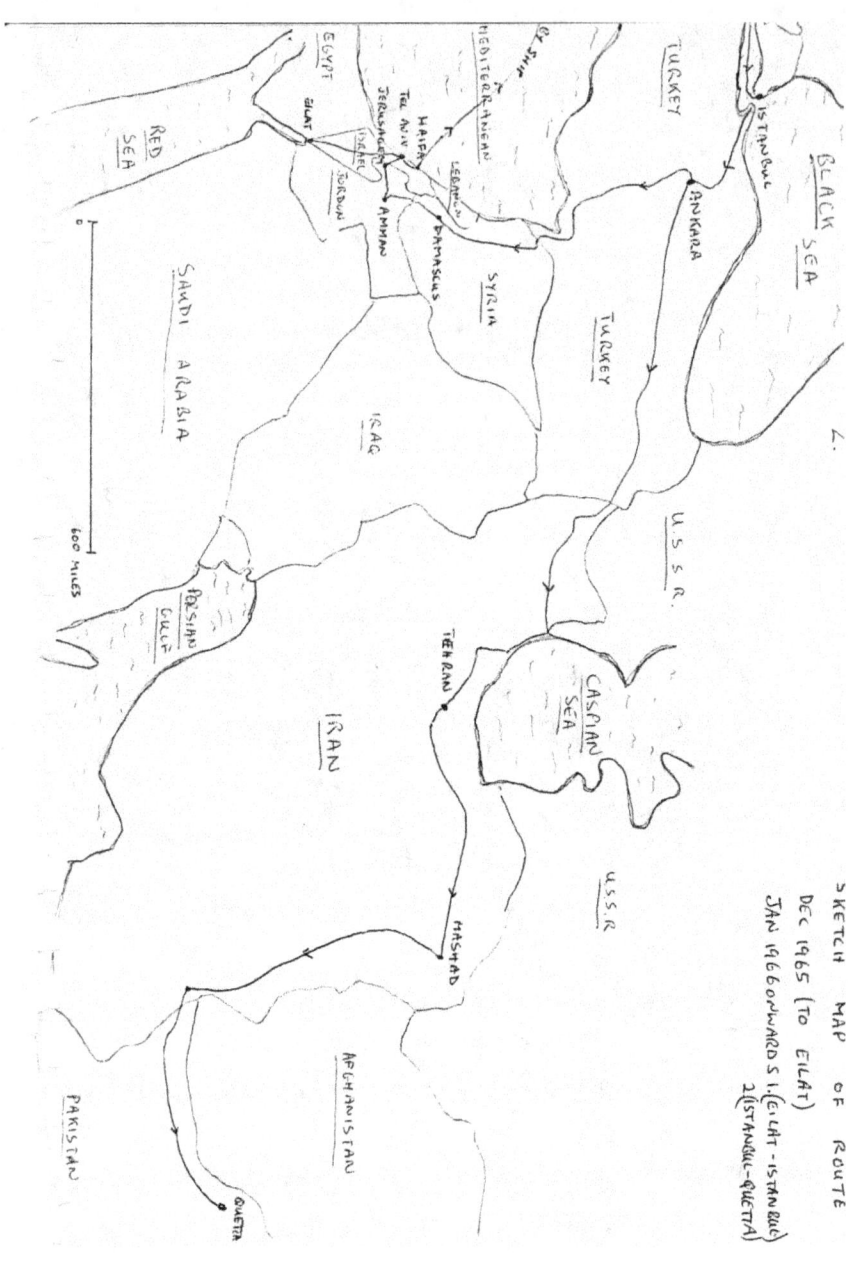

CHAPTER TWO
A Long Way from Home

I was dropped off in Istanbul near to the Blue Mosque area. This district had become a well - known haven for the international hippy set, and contained a variety of very cheap hotels, as well as innumerable teashops. Sweet puddings were a preferred delicacy of the young travelers, and accordingly one favorite meeting place was known as the "Pudding Shop". This and one or two other teahouses were the rendezvous points for the foreign back packers and itinerants in Istanbul. People would gather here to discuss the merits of traveling in India, Nepal, Israel and Greece. Tips were freely exchanged on the subjects of visas, immunization, ways to travel without money, and on the availability of hashish. (Cannabis resin).

Before I checked into one of the local bed bug infested hotels, I changed some money and began to sample the foodstuffs offered by the numerous street kiosks and stalls. There were an incredible number of food items, which for me then had a strange and wondrous novelty. Sweets, savories, kebabs or yogurts: all were very cheap. It was always the sweet things that seemed to delight me, as they did so many other young travelers. I wonder how many visitors to foreign lands, which provide new food sensations, are able to satisfy some of their unfulfilled childhood wishes of indulging in endless sweet treats?

I remember as a child having dreams in which I had the free run of a sweet-shop. That was so much more satisfying to me than the idea of being let loose in a bank or in a jewelers. I kept my sweet tooth for another ten or so years, when a preference for savory things took over completely.

By arriving in Istanbul, I had passed one of the barriers, which divides East and West. Everything was so cheap, so affordable - even for someone with so little money. Prices were about a tenth of those in England, and probably I could have spent a whole winter in Istanbul on my fifteen pounds. One of the major attractions for the hippy community was the cheapness and availability of hashish. Hashish was almost legitimate then in Istanbul, and it was only later that the huge influx of young buyers and users caused the government to impose restrictions. The crackdown was very harsh when it came, and is epitomised in the film "Midnight Express".

I began to smoke a lot of hashish in the dingy hotels where European and American hippies stayed. I used this drug on and off for nearly a year, until I reached India. In India, I was to give up not only hashish, but also smoking, alcohol and meat - eating. However, for a while my behavior was heavily influenced by the hippy culture of the people with whom I mixed. My experience of that culture of drug use was not all negative, as in some ways I feel that it helped me to get a lot of frustration out of my system. Also I am now aware of the dangers of even so called innocuous drugs, like cannabis, which can cause severe damage. Of course, with heavy use alcohol is as bad as "soft" drugs; and either can be equally damaging. One of the side aspects of hashish smoking in Istanbul was the proximity and exposure to "heavier" drugs and their users. Not all young travelers I met at that time used drugs, of course, but it did seem to be the majority culture. Some I met were using opium, and amongst the Americans, L.S.D. use was common. Later in India I was to find that many of the converts to Indian sects and gurus had been regular L.S.D. users.

In this case, some change may have occurred after the experience of mystical states through use of the drug. Did this then lead to a turning to religion for a more permanent high? Other drug users who were turned towards the easy availability of morphine, opium, and a myriad of substances, (especially in Kabul), did not always return home alive, or if they did it was to end up in psychiatric hospitals.

At the time, I had no clear opinions as to the rightness or otherwise of the morals and philosophy of the restless band that appeared in the sixties and seventies - the flower power children, the Beatniks and the hippies. The question I now ask is what the so-called Western progress of that time was doing about creating a better society to live in, as we produced so many grownup but disillusioned "war babies". More importantly though, I query the world wide same continuing trends in respect of today's young people.

In Istanbul I learnt of other hippy centers and of places where it was "all happening". One such place was at Eilat, a town at the southernmost tip of Israel, on the shores of the Red Sea. One had to travel through Turkey, via Ankara, and then into Syria and Jordan, before reaching the then Israeli border in Jerusalem. I was told that if I decided to make the trip, I should tell no Arab that I was on my way to Israel. Also, I would not be able to return out of Israel into Jordan by land, and would have to get a boat out. However, I had heard that work was available on a casual basis in and around Eilat, and that I should be able to earn enough to return home to England.

I met an American guy named Bill who was already planning to hitchhike to Israel, and I teamed up with him to make the journey. We set out from Istanbul, having taken the ferry across the Bosphorus, and were soon on our way towards the snow-covered mountains that straddled the route to Ankara. After two fascinating weeks in Istanbul, I was now ready to travel further afield. Although it was my first trip abroad, the impact of bazaars and mosques had faded quickly.

The scenery through the mountains was magnificent, but standing by the road in the snow waiting for lifts, spoiled the effect. After a cold day's travel, we had to sleep in freezing hotel beds infested by bed bugs, which left itchy red wheals as their "visiting cards". Bed bugs, mosquitoes and "germs "were, and still are, the bane of the budget traveler in the East. For all the interesting experiences the poor countries of the East provide, there are equally unpleasant surprises lying in wait for the foreign traveler. Of course the visitor who stays in deluxe class facilities can avoid a lot of discomfort, but then misses out on the unique flavor and atmosphere of the country visited.

As we traveled on through Ankara and down into Syria, we began to find that the local people we met were becoming more and more hospitable. We realized that the Turk (or Arab), has the welfare of a guest in mind in his conversation, and would also be keen to help. It was because of this "Oriental philosophy" and practice of hospitality that later on I was able to travel further and further east with absolutely no money. There is a great sense of responsibility towards the visitor. Often people would strike up a conversation and invite us for a meal in their home, or offer to show us something of some local place of interest, or aspect of their life and culture.

We made rapid progress south, stopping for the nights in Aleppo, Damascus and Amman. To me then, towns and cities were just places on the way to wherever I was going, and I was not interested in looking round and doing the things that tourists do. Even Jerusalem and the Holy Land had little meaning for me, as I was keener to meet up with fellow travelers, smoke "joints" of cannabis, and discuss the destination ahead. I feel that I was always looking ahead, because I hoped that I would reach somewhere in the world where my inner questions would be answered. All the time, though, I did not know what I was searching for, or even why I was searching. Nevertheless, I was certainly not traveling with a tourist's outlook, and the meanings of great and magnificent places were completely lost on me. I was in another world really, which may seem strange to a more mature person, but then I was just turning eighteen, and very unaware of what was driving me.

The first lift we got out of Jerusalem took us towards Tel Aviv along a winding road through the hills. Our truck driver pointed out hulks of military, and other, vehicles by the side of the road. These were reminders of the time when the Arabs had had control over the surrounding hills, and when taking convoys up to Jerusalem was a dangerous business. That day happened to be Christmas Day 1965, and the first of my Christmases overseas and away from home. It was also the day after my birthday, which had been a non-event. We celebrated with some oranges, provided by our friendly truck driver. I did not miss Christmas, as I was only too glad to be absolved and away from it. I had never really appreciated the ritual of present giving and receiving, nor the financial and other burdens that many people suffer at Christmas time. The parties and the food were fine, (but then one can enjoy such pleasures of life any time one chooses).

The way to Eilat lay down through the Negev desert, and was to be crossed by hitching a lift on one of the huge trucks that plied this route. As we went south, so the bitter cold climate of a central Turkey winter was left behind as an old memory. We changed to the warmth of cloudless days. No wonder that Eilat was the winter home then favored by the rootless young, the backpackers, and the hippy fraternity.
I stayed the first few days in the youth hostel at Eilat. Two events of those days remain in my memory. Firstly, my money finally ran out: the fifteen pounds had lasted over a month. Secondly, I gave up shaving and have not shaved my beard myself to this day. The youth hostel was on the southern edge of town, where the desert began. Close nearby, in a natural amphitheatre amongst the hills, was a camp of tents and flimsy huts that had been built of scrap wood, cardboard and polythene. These were the homes of the hippy community: people who had arrived here from different countries such as Britain, America, Germany, Sweden, and even Colombia and Brazil. The size of the place varied with the number of residents, which at that time consisted of thirty or forty souls. Some of the tents and huts were not owned by anyone in particular, as their original occupiers had moved on elsewhere and left them behind. I wandered into the camp, made friends, and found that I could have a small tent all to myself if I

wished. The guy who owned it was just moving on, and did not want the bother of carrying it, as he was heading East, where he said he would not need it.

Some of the camp dwellers had been in Eilat for several months and had casual jobs: working in the Sulphur mines, loading trucks, digging holes, or whatever. There was plenty of casual work available due to the expansion and construction of the town, which was also developing as a tourist resort. Somebody would wander into the camp and say that they wanted two people for four hours, or something like that, and one would get paid by the hour. A few people had got more permanent jobs in the hotels by the sea, or in one of the restaurants. They would usually bring "home" items of food, (mostly left-overs), for the communal cook pot, which meant that the lazy could always find something to eat in the camp. I quickly discovered one of the easier ways of earning a crust in Eilat. This was bottle collecting. There was money to be had from taking empty bottles (beer, lemonade, etc.), back to the shops and there always seemed to be "empties" lying around on the beach, or in the town litter bins. A few hours scrounging around for bottles usually provided enough money to buy a loaf of bread and a bottle of milk, and sometimes enough to sit in a cafe as well.

One guy showed me his own unique system of bottle collecting. He took me out at night through the dry sandy gullies to the back of town where yards full of crates of empties were kept. The fences around the, yard had their weak points arid it proved easy to remove a few crates over or under the wire. Those crates of empties, once hidden in a suitable gully, provided the means to buy a small feast to last a week. My conscience was not always easy about this so I took up other work.

One of the problems with the various casual jobs was the difficulty in getting paid, as most of the employers seemed reluctant to hand over the money. They were always trying to get as much work out of people for as little outlay as possible. I think the locals quite despised the inhabitants of the camp, but because they needed plenty of work animals, we were tolerated and allowed to stay.

In the warm winter of Eilat I could have existed quite easily on a little bottle collecting now and then. However I needed money to travel further; at least enough for the boat fare back to Istanbul. I began to travel on the daily bus to the local Sulphur mines, where I could work any day and also get a large free meal at the end of the shift. It was dirty, backbreaking work, involving shoveling Sulphur into sacks for hours on end. Some of the regulars from the camp had better and more responsible jobs. One of them was a strange character who looked like a cross between a scarecrow and a chimney sweep. He never washed or changed his clothes and, although his appearance was shocking, he spoke softly and seemed a well-educated person. I thought that perhaps he was doing a sort of penance to atone for his past sins. He seemed to have that kind of religious fervor in his personality.

The camp was a friendly place to live, as in the evening everyone would gather around a wood fire, passing round bowls of hot stew, along with a seemingly endless supply of joints. I heard stories and tales of travel from people who had been to Nepal, Afghanistan and India. I learnt that one could live in these places on next to nothing or without money at all. The people there were friendly and hospitable towards the penniless hippy, and had totally different attitudes from those of the Western civilizations. I learnt also that the more one tried to adopt Eastern habits and customs, the greater a welcome one received.

For many people in Asia it was, and still is, a great source of comfort that people from all the powerful, materialistic, Christian countries of the West should be interested in adopting their lifestyles and philosophies. That an Englishman should come into their midst and sit on the floor and eat with his right hand: this alone enormously pleased many people in the Asian homes I later visited. In India they had been used to the rulers of the British Raj; people who often showed little regard for the native Indian customs, practices and beliefs. Small wonder then that when the first hippies arrived in the East, they were lavished with affection and hospitality, that is, until the arrival of masses of them. When the native population of India, Afghanistan and other countries found that a lot of hippies were selfish and heavily drug orientated, then their feelings of goodwill were soured. In the sixties though, before the massive influx on the overland trail, a lot of travelers were genuinely converted by the cultures with which they came into contact, and tried to give as much as they could in return for the hospitality they received.

As I heard about the wonders of the overland trail to India, and of the wonderful lifestyle that could be found, so I decided that my return to Istanbul would be just a stop on my route eastwards. I was not going back to England, even if it meant traveling with an empty pocket and, (in Muslim) terms, relying on the will of Allah for my sustenance.

After a couple of months at the camp in Eilat I had to leave, along with everyone else. The order had come from the town hall, and police had been sent to make sure that the huts and tents were pulled down. The event did not seem to bother a lot of the camp residents as it made the decision for them of whether to stay or travel onwards. Some, including me, retreated into the hills for a few weeks to stay in a small group of three huts, hidden in the ravines. We had a long walk to get to our nearest tap water, but otherwise it was fine as we were not bothered, even though we went into town.

Whilst I was there I experimented with belladonna tobacco. One is supposed to smoke this tobacco for asthma relief, but some bright spark had discovered that when eaten, it produces interesting hallucinatory effects. The "approved" method was to swallow a few spoonfuls of the stuff late at night and then go to sleep until the effects began. I tried some, washed down with lemonade, and woke up early in the morning with a shock. I felt that I was entombed, or as if in a womb and had to struggle to get outside the hut. During all that day I saw "forms" that appeared to be those of my mother, father, and people from my childhood memories. Later in the day, I saw Roman troops marching on the hill tops and a train coming out of the ravine: Other people who had tried belladonna this way said that they had also had experiences of regression to childhood memories similar to my own.

The after effects of belladonna were unpleasant, badly affecting my vision and bladder. The experience had been very interesting though, and I could see why people took mind expanding drugs like L.S.D. This was my first strong experience of another reality, separate from the world I saw around me daily. Hashish had given me some idea of altered consciousness states, but not on this level. It was, however, a dangerous world to venture into, and I decided to avoid the hallucinogenics. Later I met travelers who had become psychotic through use of these drugs; people who would have been committed to a psychiatric hospital had they been in England.

During our last few weeks in Eilat, we found that the army had left behind a pile of unused supplies near us, in one of their temporary camp sites. There was a pile of loaves of bread that had dried out in the sun, but proved quite edible. We also found some large, unopened cans of jam, a quantity of (dubious) hard-boiled eggs and (equally dubious), a few live hand grenades:

That was my last memory of Eilat, before hitch hiking to Tel Aviv to get a student card in order to buy a cheap boat ticket. The people at the student offices in Tel Aviv must have issued dozens of student cards over a few days to ex Eilat campers. There certainly seemed to be no objection to granting dozens of passes which gave a fifty per cent reduction on the Haifa to Istanbul boat fare. Perhaps there was some official collusion to assist us in leaving the country, because we had been living in a sensitive area on the Egyptian border. (Eilat is also a mile from Aquaba on the Red Sea in Jordan). That border was rolled back a year later in 1967 when the Israelis made their moves of the Six Day War.

From Tel Aviv I hitched to Haifa with a friend, and went to sell my blood. It was my first experience of giving blood, and I was surprised at how weak I felt afterwards. I think I received the equivalent of three pounds, which was quite a lot when the boat fare to Istanbul was only five pounds, (after a fifty per cent discount). With this money and what I had left from my toil at the Sulphur works, I felt fairly affluent. I knew that quite a few young travelers sold their blood frequently. A popular place was Kuwait, which was, perhaps surprisingly, one of the favored destinations for overland travelers. One got a good price for blood there, enough perhaps to buy a deck class ticket on the British East India Company ships to Pakistan and India.

After giving blood and feeding ourselves on yoghurt and sweet pastries, we found a convenient park in which to pass the night whilst waiting our ship's departure. I think the crew of the ship got the shock of their lives when they found about two dozen grubby, long haired or barefoot youths waiting to ascend the gangway to take up their cabins. The immediate novelty of the ship for most of us was the proper meal arrangements, on well-set tables. Unfortunately for me, I was sea sick for the first twenty four hours and was annoyed that I could not eat the unaccustomed square-meals.

On the ship amongst us were two Austrian lads who had been to India, and had lived with begging bowls in the temples. One of them had been affected by drug use and was in a catatonic and psychotic state. He hardly spoke. He sat or lay motionless most of the time, and had to be fed by his friend. The ship's doctor had a look at him and gave him an injection, which seemed to bring him to life for a few hours. The Austrians were on their way back home, and I often wondered what happened to them. They would be fiftyish today and could be in psychiatric care, or successful businessmen, or even social workers. Who knows?

On the way to Istanbul, the temperatures became cooler and we realized that winter was no yet over in this part of the world. On the ship I had made some friends who were going to live on a small island a ferry ride from Galata Bridge in Istanbul. On this island, a wealthy Turk had turned over the use of his summer chalet to poor foreign travelers.

Istanbul was in the grips of foul, sleety weather when we arrived. I think it was early March but I am not sure, as by then I had lost track of the days, the weeks and even the months.

It did not seem particularly important to me then that I did not have a watch, nor keep a diary, nor take photographs. The whole purpose of my travels was to free myself from what I felt were the encumbrances that society tried to impose on me. I was not aware of what was happening in the world, and was not interested either. I did not bother to read newspapers or listen to the radio, even if I had the chance.

I went to stay on the little island of which I had heard. It was a cheap ferry ride away, and one of a number of islands off Istanbul. It had a small village facing the jetty and harbor, behind which were several square miles of hilly land dotted with summer holiday chalets. I found the chalet where a group of ten or so young travelers had their home. Why the owner had opened up his chalet for the use of a band of scruffy wanderers, I do not know. Certainly such sympathy was welcome, especially as the chalet had a wood stove which kept the place nice and warm. Unfortunately we burnt some of the wrong wood: planks that were to be used for repairs, and the owner nearly threw us all out. On the stove we always had hot water for drinks. Someone had donated several large drums of milk powder which, in turn, had been donated by America to impoverished Turkey.

There was always enough money for the cheap ferry into the city and some sort of food, mainly bread, to eat at the chalet. Everyone was willing to share a little of the "windfalls" of cash, which came from parents at home, from jobs, and from the sale of blood. A person who could afford to go to the city restaurants for a meal would usually bring back a few loaves of bread for the kitty. Thus those who were down on their monetary resources could survive until something turned up. The Americans always appeared the most affluent. They seemed to be continually receiving money from home, whereas the rest mostly had to earn somehow whatever they got. Having returned to Istanbul again, I suppose that I should have headed home in order to get a job, earn some money and/or save for my next trip. However, all that I had imbibed of the East, (that is, India and Nepal), had fired me with such enthusiasm to head in that direction, that I knew I could survive without money as others had done. The tales of living in India with a begging bowl and subsisting on a handful of rice had stirred something within me. The whole culture of the mystical mendicant - the *sadhu* was pulling me like a magnet. I had a need to discover something that I could not get by living and working in England. The way of the *sadhu*, even though involving a lot of renunciation of pleasures and comforts, actually seemed to me to be a pleasant sort of way to live.

Mantra - a Sanskrit symbolic word for repetition or chanting.

It is a paradox that is not easily explained. Generally humans struggle for material wellbeing, yet many seek out "unnecessary" hardships in spiritual endeavor, in mountain climbing and arduous expeditions, or in selfless voluntary work.

India had caught my attention as a child. I had read avidly the books of Jim Corbett, in which he tracked down man-eating tigers. Some such tigers had killed hundreds of humans over several years, and his book about the Man - Eating Tigers of Kumaon was outstanding in my mind. Although animals were killed in his stories, I felt that he lived a special, spiritual life, in tune with the jungle. Nowadays his name is given to an Indian National Park, and is linked with the preservation of India's tigers.

Years later in India, I was to have a strange dream in which I was an Englishman tiger hunting in the jungle. I met a sadhu, who seemed to emanate light, sitting on a grassy bank outside a cave. I went into the cave with this sadhu and became an initiate of his, receiving a holy mantra. I left my gun in the cave and came out vowing never to hunt animals again. My Indian teacher at that time, who interpreted this dream, said it meant that in my previous birth I had been an

Englishman in India: possibly a government official living in a forest area with good hunting. I had, according to him, been initiated into Hindu meditation and yoga practices in that life. Also the reason I had returned to India was to complete the *sadhana,* (practice), I had thus previously begun. Even as a child in England I had read some books on yoga and meditation. For a while I had tried the meditation method of concentrating on a spot on the wall, as advised in one of the books. However nothing came of it at the time, and it seemed to have been a passing interest

I had heard from friends in the Istanbul chalet that there was a way of getting to Tehran, not only for free, but with an added profit also. This was achieved by helping an Iranian import a deluxe model car from Germany to Iran. One had to become the temporary owner of the car, on paper at least, so that the Iranian could get around some of the import duties and regulations which existed then. Quite a few people were involved in this "trade", and one only had to visit certain hotels in the city to make all the arrangements. The benefits to me would be a free ride to Tehran, plus ten pounds or so, in local money, paid in Tehran when the car was signed back to the Iranians.

I soon met two Iranians in a hotel in the city. They had bought a Mercedes in Germany and would require nothing more from me than signature on some papers in order to make the trip with the car in my name. The "ownership" of the car was also later written in my passport at the Iranian border, with the number and other details being entered in Arabic script.

The three of us set off one morning from the European aide of Istanbul, and crossed the Bosphorus to the Asian side. We headed east for a stretch of solid driving, broken only by meal and hotel stops at night. The two Iranians were friendly enough, but did seem to be in a hurry as they daily drove from sunrise to sunset almost non- stop. Part of the deal was that I got well fed en-route, and to their irritation I used to complain if we did not have proper lunch stops.

After protracted delays at the Turkish and Iranian border posts, which involved considerable wrangling, mostly, it seemed over the customary bribe money, we entered Iran.

Having paid our dues we drove off at a much more leisurely pace, taking the northern route towards at the edge of Russia's empire, and the Caspian Sea. I remember driving past a border fence, passing fences with ominous looking towers jutting high up in the trees behind. I developed one of my innumerable Asian tummy bugs, and the two Iranians went out of their way to find suitable restaurant food for me. They had become much friendlier since entering Iran and now seemed to be in no rush to get anywhere.

The two Iranians ran a photographic shop in Tehran and they invited me to stay with their respective families for a while. I ended up staying few weeks, and was given marvelous tours of the city and surroundings. They and their families became very affectionate towards me, although there was in the beginning a rather absurd incident. One of the Iranians took me to his home late at night. Shortly after I arrived at the house, before I met the family, there developed a furious argument in the next room between him and the women of the house. The mother of my friend had seen my boyish figure and long hair from the back through a window in faint light and had assumed that her son was bringing home a girl he had picked up off the streets. The upshot was that my friend was kicked out for that night and we both had to sleep in the car. Apparently long hair on men in was unusual those parts. Even though had a short beard, they perhaps did not see it in the dim light or thought it was a disguise. Later I returned to the house and they accepted that I was indeed a male.

The only other problem I encountered in Tehran concerned the car, I had to go with my two Iranian friends to a large police headquarters to be interviewed by a senior policeman about certain irregularities. I was asked if I knew that the car had been stolen in Munich. The policeman had a lot of car registration numbers, which had been sent from Germany, although I believe that my friends had bought the car in good faith. Strangely, without any particular explanation on my part, we were ushered out and, before going home, visited the police car compound. The Mercedes was surrounded by dozens of similar vehicles. Next day I found myself being shown more tourist spots by my happy friends in the Mercedes. Judging by their cheerfulness, I could only assume that the affair had not cost them too much.

My departure from Tehran was accompanied by fond farewells from my friends at the crowded bus station. Here I saw for the first time groups of pious Muslim pilgrims who were coming back from Mecca. I think a lot of them were returning to Afghanistan, as they seemed a different type of person from the Persians. They had coarser, simpler clothes and a rougher, rugged appearance. I had a ticket to Mashad, a big town two hundred miles from the Afghan border, plus some money in my pocket and a packed lunch. So far, I had done quite well with my journey towards India and Nepal.
On the bus I found that I was the center of interest. The other travelers were keen to see how I would behave when we stopped for meal and toilet breaks on the two - day journey. I was beginning to learn Asian customs, such as using the right hand for eating, and the left for wiping the bottom whilst splashing on water from a can. Using toilet paper was considered a very dirty habit by these Moslems, so I tried to copy what I saw the men around me doing, and collected a special can with a spout from the places where we stopped.

The men on the bus wanted to chat to me, and by using signs and a few simple words. I was able to convey to them my general direction and purpose. Everywhere we stopped, I was offered a meal or tea, and whilst on the move fruit would be passed to me. I found it incredibly difficult to refuse the very sweet tea which was frequently offered to me, so I drank gallons of the stuff, even though I disliked it. This bus ride was the real beginning of my experience of genuine hospitality from all quarters of the public around me as I traveled further and further east. Until then I had received much goodwill and help, but now I was beginning to find it difficult sometimes to politely decline gifts and offers of food. Often my refusal was not accepted and I was almost forced to eat or drink something - difficult if my tummy was not behaving like a local.

    I had planned to travel across Afghanistan to Pakistan, and accordingly visited the Afghani embassy in Mashad to get a visa. I had to fill out a form which asked for my details and required me to state how much money I had. Unthinkingly I entered five pounds or so for my financial status, and found that I could not have a visa. They wanted to give visas to proper tourists with a hundred dollars or so in their pockets at least. I realized immediately that I should have written a suitable sum on the form hoping that they would not ask to see the actual money.

    Being unable to enter Afghanistan, I decided to go around it, with a journey of some eight hundred miles to Zehedan in the south being my first stage. Then, after crossing into Pakistan, I would have to travel up the whole length of that country to reach Lahore. After a night in a Mashad hotel I bought a bus ticket some way south, leaving myself with the equivalent of a few pounds for emergency food needs.

    I traveled to a small town by late afternoon, walked to the outskirts and stood waiting to hitch a lift. The people on the bus had been puzzled when they found out that I intended to go further south, but was getting off the bus at this small town. They seemed to be talking of having a whip-a-round" so that I could continue, but I felt embarrassed by this and made some lame excuses, explaining that I needed to have a break in my journey.

    I was sitting by the road waiting to see if I could get a lift before nightfall, when I was approached by two young men wheeling bicycles. They knew some English and began to ask me what I was doing, in this isolated spot. They told me that I could catch a bus in town, or if I liked there was a reasonable hotel in which to spend the night. When I tried to explain that I could not afford either a hotel or the bus to Zahedan, some six hundred miles distant, they seemed quite upset. They told me to go to a large house nearby and seek help. However I was quite happy where I was as I had enough money for several days' food, and if necessary I would spend the night out in the warm air by the roadside. After telling them of my intentions, they seemed satisfied and cycled off.

A little while later they returned with a policeman who asked me to accompany him to the police station. There I was introduced to the boss who asked me a few questions about my financial state, using the two young men, who had followed, as interpreters. This head of the station had a look at my passport, wrote something on some official paper, and passed it to the two young men. He said, "Hotel, hotel", and bade that I accompany the men into town. I hoped that because of a misunderstanding.

I was not being shunted off to a hotel where I would have to explain my penniless state all over again. I had met "helpful" people before who refused to believe that I could travel without plenty of money stashed away somewhere. They usually shunned me as if I had the plague when they eventually found out that I really was in a state of poverty.

However, my new found helpers told me that I was being accommodated for free at the town's hotel. Not only that, I was to have a free meal and breakfast, and the following day they would take me to the bus stand where I would get a free ride to Zahedan. I was told that I was not just receiving the goodwill of the local citizens, but there was a government resource for tourists in distress.

At that time, they had not become used to a steady flow of hippies and others on the overland trail.

No doubt a few years later, after the boom of the Flower Power Era influx of pilgrims to the drug centers of the Orient, the locals developed far less benevolent views. I was told that a group of eight Europeans had been helped previously on this route. How eight people could hitch-hike together, I did not understand, although later I was to travel in a group of four. In those kindly days any thing was possible for travelers but it was, however, much easier for a single male. I knew that girls traveled the overland route - usually with a male. For them, life could be difficult. Females from the West were often then in dire danger in Asian countries due to the obnoxious and sometimes threatening advances of the local male population. Even traveling with a male partner did not protect the females from much harassment. Often the male partner was threatened or, more usually, offered money for the services of "his" woman.

Asian men had a strict culture then, in terms of how they behave with their own women. Free contacts are restricted to the women in one's own family and any other female has to be treated with caution and respect. However, then, when foreign girls came into their country, some of the local men lost all sense of decency and behaved like a pack of wolves. They assumed that all women traveling in hippy style must be "loose" - and behaved accordingly. Some countries are worse than others in this respect. Generally, the stricter their own moral code with regard to women, the more outrageous their men were with regard to female hippy travelers from Westernized countries.

I reached Zahedan after several days' free bus travel, courtesy of the Iranian government, and set off on the desert road to the Pakistan border at Nor Lundi. Obliging truck drivers brought me to the border post, which was a collection of thatched huts in the middles of nowhere. The only formality then was to get a stamp in my passport and show customs my A had then only small bag containing a spare shirt, a towel and a few other items. I had long since given away all the heavy clothes, as I did not require them for summer in this part of the world. I kept a pair of leather shoes in my bag, however, and used cheap sandals for my feet.

At the border I met an English guy who was on his way to Quetta, in Pakistan, to see about buying a block of hashish, which he intended to smuggle back to England. Some three hundred miles northwards, Quetta was at that time quite a center for hashish buyers from Europe, most of them of the amateurish type. I hitch- hiked there with the English guy, and he let me stay in his hotel room for a few days. We visited the local tea shops where we were made most welcome, being served without charge, tea, sweets, and hookahs filled with tobacco and hashish. I was surprised at how freely the hashish trade and use went on in this town - but then it was situated in a very independent area of Pakistan not far from the Afghanistan border. In those days, one could buy opium legally from shops in the Indian subcontinent, not to speak of the cheaply available hashish. After all, cannabis plants grew wild to a great height on plots of vacant land around the towns and villages.

Quetta was a Wild West type town, with roguish looking fellows strolling in the streets, often with a rifle over their shoulders. Outside the banks sat heavily mustachioed men with shotguns draped across their laps, ready to protect the probably not inconsiderable sums of money and gold inside. I drank bhang in this town for the first time. It is a concoction made carefully from the leaves of the female cannabis plant and is mixed with ground cardamom, almonds, sugar and spice. I fell asleep in the park for a whole day after drinking the stuff in the morning; an event which caused much hilarity amongst the locals. This heady brew also gave me a raging appetite and some of my new - found Quetta friends obligingly treated me to a sweet shop feast.

I set off yet again, this time for Lahore and the Indian border, some five hundred miles northwards. I got a series of lift from friendly lorry drivers who not only brought me nearer to my destination, but often bought me meals at the way - side ramshackle cafes they frequented. The trucks would park outside these cafes at night and the drivers would be given a charpoy to spend the night on in the warm open air. I too was made welcome in these often boisterous eating - places and frequently treated to the best *charpoy*. (A bed made of rope strung between a wooden frames). I preferred the firm ground to that rickety and uncomfortable bed.

Thus I arrived in Lahore, and met the two Swedes whose temporary "home" was the local jail. I had reached the Indian border, but unfortunately it was closed. I began my trek back to England after giving way to a feeling that attempts to reach India could be hopeless. I did reach India as it turned out, but only after a journey first westwards into Afghanistan, and then back to Quetta whilst en-route to Karachi.

CHAPTER THREE
Last Years as an Englishman

The two Swedes told me all about traveling in India and Pakistan without a ticket. They said that if a, ticket collector came along, you just pleaded poverty and most of them would let you stay on the train. Not only that, but the other passengers would often be very helpful when they knew you were traveling ticket less. This only applied in third class, where the average passenger was fairly poor and sympathetic to fare dodgers generally. However, if people saw that you had money, a camera, or even a watch, then not only could you be branded as a fake, but you attracted the attention of passengers who were interested in your property. I was also told that some stationmasters were very friendly to penniless travelers and had in the past given "chits" to people so they could get a free ride. Nowadays in this part of the world, ticket less travel can mean jail - whether you are European, poor, a holy - man, or whatever.

    I went along to Lahore station aiming to catch the train to Peshawar, where I could get an Afghan visa and head off up the Khyber Pass. The stationmaster was on the platform just outside his office, so I went up to him and asked him if it was all right to get on the train without a ticket, as I did not have any money. He seemed to understand my English, and waved at me to get on the train as it was just leaving.

Peshawar was some four hundred miles away, so I settled down for a couple of days train ride. My fellow travelers in the carriage soon became curious about me and wanted to know all my details and particulars. I was getting used to this style of conversation by now, and if someone came up and asked me how my bowels were working, then 1 was not surprised: In this part of the world it was quite the norm to be asked questions concerning my marital status, job, wage, family, eating habits and so forth. And that was from people who had never seen me before, who just came over and introduced themselves. However, the questions I was asked were posed by polite well-wishers who, when they heard my story, would often offer me food or even money.

Some of the local people I met were full of admiration for my lifestyle, saying that I had surrendered to the will of Allah for my food and lodging needs, and that I was a spiritually minded person. I was indeed rapidly becoming a believer in a God of some sort, otherwise the uncertainty of my day to day life would have sent me fleeing to the nearest British High Commission asking to be repatriated. Once a non-believer, now if anyone asked me where my next meal or shelter was coming from, I would say, "It is God's will", and look up to the heavens.

Whilst on the train, one educated English speaking Pakistani criticized me heavily for the type of life I was leading. He then asked me if I had eaten lunch, and when I said I had not, he offered to buy me some. I declined but he ordered one for me anyway from the waiters who came around at midday. When the food was brought to me, other interested passengers gathered round. They all seemed to derive great pleasure from watching this long haired, shabbily dressed foreigner tucking into their native dishes with great gusto. They nudged each other to point to my use of the right hand, giving nods of approval at the same time. I felt a bit like an animal in the zoo at feeding time. Once they had seen that I liked their type of food, the other shyer non English speaking passengers competed to buy me tea and tidbits from stations at which we later stopped.

One ticket collector came around half way through my journey, but did not seem concerned that I had no ticket. Just before Peshawar, however, another collector appeared and became quite upset when I said I had been on the train since Lahore. He told me that I would have to stay on the train in Peshawar station while he investigated my case. I presumed he meant to get a railway policeman, and, not wishing to end up in jail (even for the free food and accommodation), I hopped off the train at a signal stop just out of town.

As I wandered into Peshawar it was becoming dark and I was wondering where I could stay. A man came up to me and started talking to me in broken English, asking me all the inevitable questions. He invited me to stay at his simple home and meet his family. As he seemed a genuinely hospitable person, I agreed. He was an off duty policeman so I felt secure in his company, although the situation was a bit ironic, considering my furtive departure from the train.

He lived with his family in a small house in a congested area of tenements and buildings that seemed fairly impoverished. I guess his salary was not much more than sufficient for the bare essentials of family life. He and his family proved very friendly and put e. lot of energy into looking after me the night I stayed. He told me about Swat valley to the north of Peshawar and said I would enjoy a visit to that area, as it was very beautiful. I decided to hitch hike there, take a look, and perhaps go up to the Chitral area, which was further into the mountains towards Afghanistan. My friendly policeman insisted that I caught the bus to Swat valley and duly accompanied me to the bus station to purchase my ticket and make sure I got a good seat. He also passed me a package containing my lunch.

I got out of the bus at the last town in the valley at which it stopped, and decided to wander out of town and look for somewhere to sleep in the open. I sat down on the parapet of a small bridge to await darkness before I bedded down for the night. I had not been there for long before a few local people came up and started asking me the usual questions. They told me I should come and stay in one of their houses which was nearby, and I was about to move off with them when two well-dressed young men cycled up rapidly.

The two young men were greeted deferentially by the other villagers, and one of the two introduced himself as the Prince of the locality. The other man was his secretary, and said in good English that I had to go along with them and be the Prince's guest for a week or so. I was not just invited, I was told that I was to be a guest, for a short while at least. I was quite happy to go along with their wishes as I rather fancied staying in a palace. The principality, however, did not amount to all that much, and the "palace" was just a large house with a number of outbuildings. My quarters turned out to be quite comfortable, a large cool room with attached bathroom, and a nice verandah overlooking a walled garden and lawn. They had some more guest rooms next to mine which were empty. I thought that perhaps they did not get many guests, especially foreigners, thus making me quite a good "catch".

The Prince was rather eccentric in my opinion. I used to see him only in the evenings in his sitting room, where we would chat. He told me that he was bothered by spirits of some sort, and asked me to write to him if I found a suitable cure in the course of my travels. He was quite keen that I should still try to visit India, as he thought that I would find there the solution for which he was looking.

During the week or so 1 spent at the "palace", I had most days free to do as I I wished. Food was brought to my room at regular hours, so other times I wandered around the local hills for a few hours. I had some hashish with me and used to find a quiet spot under some trees where I surreptitiously rolled myself a joint.

For a week or so as I had been suffering from for intermittent diarrhea so I was happy to rest up. I was able to see a doctor as well and get some medicine, and obtain some bland food for a change.

The Prince did not seem to be well off considering his status, or perhaps he was just economizing. He had no car, few servants, and his house was sparsely furnished. He did, however, have his own private prison. Every morning, a number of men in chains would clank past my room on their way to some earth works near the garden. The prisoners did not appear to be unhappy as they were chatting away merrily when they passed by. Perhaps the Prince's jail was a cushy number compared with the State ones.

Before I left Swat valley I was given the chance of a day's ride in a lorry going northwards towards Chitral and back. A breed of rugged mountain people lived up there, often passing an individual and isolated existence. We stopped in a few villages where I attracted lots of attention. I had a pleasant day journeying through mountain gorges full of the sound of roaring rivers

White skinned visitors had become rare in these parts since the demise off the Raj. Later in Afghanistan I met people who had never seen a white person, (like me), before. There I was assumed to be either American or Russian, as engineers from those two countries were working on the Kabul - Herat road at that time.

In order to leave Swat, I had to persuade the Prince that I really needed to be on my way, and I had been a guest for long enough. I was reluctantly allowed to leave, after being given a bus ticket back to Peshawar and a hamper of food which included a whole cooked chicken.

I was able to stay for a few nights in a hotel when I arrived in Peshawar, courtesy of a small gift of money from the Prince. I made sure I got my Afghanistan entry visa this time by writing on the application form that I had one hundred American dollars. I had enough money left to catch the bus up the Khyber Pass from Peshawar to the frontier, and disembarked there for the border formalities.

The border guards were surprised that I was not continuing on with the through bus to Kabul, and they could not understand my wish to hitch hike from the border. I did not tell them I was penniless: However, I was not stopped and was able to walk up the road into Afghanistan. Several trucks full of men standing at the back were passing me and I assumed that this was an alternative to the bus service, which meant that they were taking fare paying passengers.

I decided to try one though, as the worst that could happen would be that I was thrown off. I got myself hauled aboard a truck with a dozen or so Afghanis standing in the back, and we bounced along for several hours until we stopped for tea at a wayside halt. 1 was offered some tea and the other passengers tried to find out if I was American or Russian. They were not quite so happy to discover that I was English as their last contacts in the past with the English had been in battle. This was of course many years before, but to them it was still an important issue. They indicated that they liked Germans and I remembered vaguely from my history knowledge that Germany and Afghanistan had a strong relationship going back quite a while. I was also approached by the driver's mate who asked for my fare money. He seemed rather offended at first when I tried to indicate that I had none. However then I turned out my pockets in front of the now incredulous onlookers, and I then received a friendly reaction and was made to sit down again. The driver's mate then went off and bought me more tea. Everyone in the teashops seemed puzzled by my penniless state and took to arguing amongst themselves, presumably as to whether or not they should abandon me in the middle of nowhere. Eventually the driver intervened, and motioned for me to get back on the truck. We bounced along until it was dark, when we stopped at another teashop.

That night I bedded down on the floor at the back of the teashop.

Food and drink had been brought to me and I found myself being treated in a friendly but cautious way by these unsophisticated villagers. For a start, the fact that I was not Moslem made me seem to be of very strange and perhaps inferior status to these people. I had not found this attitude in Pakistan or other countries where they had a lot of contact with non-Moslem peoples. However, in Afghanistan I was to find many village people who were bemused by the fact that I was not a Moslem. Although the Afghani people are very serious about their duties to a guest or a stranger, their generous hospitality towards me was often mixed with a circumspect approach, because they did not comprehend my beliefs. However, when they realized I was going around their country without money, they became almost proud of me. This was because they strongly believe that Allah takes care of one's needs and that one should surrender to him. Here 1 was, literally putting myself in Allah's hands. Allah was the warp and weft of their whole life and, unlike some Moslem countries, in Afghanistan everything and everyone stopped for the five times daily prayers.

Back on the road, through the rugged mountain scenery we began our winding descent to Kabul, arriving there at midday. I had completed the rest of the journey sitting in the cab, instead of standing at the back.   I had been passed tobacco, cigarettes and *churus* (cannabis resin), and at the end of the journey, enough money to buy myself lunch was pressed into my palm by the truck driver.

I entered a clingy cafe and bought myself a dish of some sort of dumplings in a curd sauce. Then I wandered into a nearby park and sat down for a rest. As a number of bystanders began to gather round me out of curiosity, I had an idea. I still carried my English leather shoes in my bag and I figured they might be worth some money here, because they were in sound condition and looked of good quality. I fished out the shoes and began waving them around in front of the onlookers, but nobody made a move forward. Shortly a young man walked up to me and asked me, in reasonable English, what I was doing. He appeared shocked on learning that I needed to sell my shoes to buy my next meal, and asked me to put them back in my bag and have tea with him. He took me to a, nearby large building, explaining that he was a dentist there in a government run institution. There I was shown his surgery, which had a modern looking dental chair as its centerpiece. He seemed quite fond of this chair, which he explained had been donated recently by a foreign government. I cannot remember if he got it from Russia or America; these were of course the two countries competing in aid giving there at the time. He explained that the new chair was not fully operative yet and had a few "bits" missing. In fact while I was there, a patient came in who had to sit in an ordinary chair in the corner whilst having some dental work done.

    The dentist invited me to stay at his family's home, which, as it turned out, was a well-appointed place in a wealthy suburb. That evening, a feast was prepared for me and I was asked to sit down on my own at the laden table, whilst all the family and some of the neighbors assembled to watch me eat. I felt embarrassed by the curious onlookers and managed to get the dentist and some of his male friends to join me. Whilst the women would not, of course, sit down with the men, this house was much more liberal than most in Afghanistan. Other houses that I ate in kept the customary *purdah,* (all-covering robes), and I never saw the women of the house. Here in this house, the women had unveiled faces and were allowed to serve up food and watch the proceedings. I have no doubt that Afghanistan had the strictest religious codes, enforced rigidly in everyday life, in comparison with other Moslem countries.

    Thus I became a "guest" once more for a few days. The dentist and several of his friends used me as a good excuse to take time off work, and showed me around some of Kabul. My most vivid memory of Kabul is not of any scenery but of one particular dish I was offered as a delicacy. It was a fried egg in a bowl, covered by an inch of oil. I did not really want to swallow the oil to get at the egg, as it seemed I was meant to do. I think that I said that I did not like eggs or something similar.

Kabul at that time was becoming a popular place for those hippies who were heavily into the drug scene. I was told by my dentist friend that they were seen as undesirable types by most Kabul people as they used the hard drugs such as opium and morphine, which were very cheap and freely available there. A hotel room and food could be had then for the equivalent of an English shilling, and several drug using Europeans had made Kabul their long term "home". I believe that quite a few of these people died at a young age in Kabul from overuse and overdose of opiates. Cannabis use seemed to be quite common in this part of the world, but alcohol was forbidden by the Moslem code. However, most educated people looked down upon cannabis use, and I cannot remember any such person offering it to me. In the tea shops and other places it was a different matter and I was continually offered and given hashish, although opium was never proffered. At that time I rather enjoyed a "smoke" in the right company, but was quite happy to be "teetotal" in more cultured houses, or in the presence of people who did not like the use of cannabis.

When, after a few days, I left Kabul, I was still heading westwards and homewards, although my immediate goal was Kandahar, some four hundred miles away. The highway then from Kabul was being built half and half by the Americans and Russians, and all along this route as I traveled for two days I found myself being asked if I was a citizen of one of these two countries. I managed to get myself lost on this route, by accepting a free bus ride that left the tarmac road and wandered off through a number of villages near the highway. The village I wound up in for the night looked like something out of a cowboy movie, only without the bars. People in this village appeared very suspicious of me and seemed to think that I was some sort of spy. Some local men led me to a kind of police station, where the officials refused to have anything to do with me and waved me away.

Then I was taken to a tea shop and shown a place where I could sleep. I was given some food and had a good night's sleep there. I think they remained a little wary of me because the usual tobacco, cigarettes or churrus were not forthcoming. Next day I got a truck ride to a tiny village further south, which was enclosed like a compound within the mud walls of a fort. I was invited in and the whole village of fifty or so souls turned out to see the strange, white skinned man in their midst. I was offered food, which consisted of a huge pile of flat bread and a tub holding, it seemed, several gallons of yogurt: It was perhaps the produce of the whole village which was being set before me, to be "blessed" by the holy guest, and thus fulfill the village's duty to Allah. They did not seem to want to scoop any of the yogurt out into a separate container for me, so I dipped the bread directly into the container, with my right hand, of course: After lunch I managed to hitch another ride back onto the highway and right into Khandahar, which is the center of an area famous for its fruit and nut production.

As I wandered into town, I found a group of young European travelers sitting on the verandah of a tea shop which had no chairs. It had a cloth and rug covered raised platform as is customary in many places in this part of the world. I joined the group of half a dozen who were reclining back on the bolsters and supping clear tea from tiny cups. I found that they were all travelers like me - insolvent to varying degrees. They had met and gathered in Khandahar mainly by chance, and now all shared two hotel rooms rented by one who had quite a lot of money. There were no objections to my having some floor space and I was included in their food sharing.

In the room I stayed I met two rather bizarre English characters who had done the overland trip before, and had taken it upon themselves to provide food for all the group. They were a mischievous and somewhat devious pair who delighted in getting all sorts of things for nothing out of the local populace. I was not too keen on their petty criminal attitude or "swashbuckling" behavior, but when they insisted they could get me to India without any problems, I decided to set off with them southwards towards Quetta, abandoning my plans of returning to England. One of the two characters called himself the "Captain" and indeed he claimed to have been one. His "mate" was a chubby guy who wore a long, dirty caftan and always had a broad grin on his face. They were quite likeable rogues really as they were willing to help out any fellow traveler if they could.

Also in my room was a Danish girl who was just recovering from a bad stomach bug. She wanted to go south towards Karachi with the intention of getting the boat to Bombay. She also decided to set off with the two "ex sailors" as they had arranged a lift on a truck to a village near the Pakistan border. In addition, they had commandeered a pile of flat bread from somewhere, so we got underway basically provisioned for the long day's journey. Near the border, we all spent the night in one room in the truck driver's house, where we slept well until a commotion woke us up in the early hours. In the darkness, the truck driver had crawled over to the Danish girl and attempted to molest her. When we lit a candle and shouted at him, he waved a knife at us, lurching around as if he was drunk. Luckily his brother came in with a lantern and dragged him outside to sort him out. Perhaps the driver had felt that as payment for our travel he should have the girl's favors, He had, though, given us the lift as a friendly gesture without trying to make any such arrangements:

The next morning, looking sheepish and embarrassed he gave us all breakfast and drove us to the border, where there were few formalities before we crossed into a little Pakistani village.

I stayed in this village another day as I had a bad case of the "runs". When I caught up with the other three, they were ensconced in a nice hotel in Quetta. I preferred to sleep in the park as 1 knew the "Captain" was up to his tricks and planned to nip off on the train without paying the hotel bill. I always get a terrible guilty conscience about doing anything illegal, and their idea of booking into a hotel without money was not my style at all. I met them again next day on the station platform as they were checking the timetable. The hotel manager also turned up as he was, rightly, suspicious of their intentions. Eventually all three of them sold their blood in Quetta and paid their way out.

I also gave my blood for money in Quetta, for the second time on my overland journey. The staff at the clinic made a mess and I got two sore and bandaged arms. These I later used to good effect on the Karachi train from Quetta, when a ticket collector was going to throw me off for ticketless travel. I pointed to my bandages and said I needed hospital treatment in Karachi. The other passengers also rallied round and in effect kicked the collector out of the compartment. I continued my journey peacefully and was well looked after by a carriage full of sympathetic Pakistanis. I managed thus to save my "blood money" for Karachi.

    I had been told of a hippy community living in beach chalets not far outside Karachi at a suburban beach resort. It was out of season there, being monsoon time, and friendly locals had turned over a number of vacant huts to itinerant travelers. The huts, I found, were floorboards, walls and roofs only - no furniture, but were being used as shelter by up to ten young people from Europe and America. Most of them were waiting for the next boat to Bombay, with money being the big question because the fare, deck class, was the equivalent of five pounds. Most of them seemed to have some cash as, in spite of their rebellion from society, money from home was providing the means of onward travel. I had some money in my pocket but it was insufficient for the boat. I used it to feed myself and an American guy I met, who was out of funds but expecting some from home.

    There was a little thatch and grass tea shop on the beach that provided us with cheap tea, *chappati* breads and *dhal* lentils, or omelets for the "millionaires" amongst the dozen or so beach dwellers. There had been a steady flow of people through the beach camp for over year, and the tea shop owner would often let people have food on credit, knowing that a little money by wire from America or England would mean a lot of rupees to be spent in his tea shop. A pound from England then would keep someone in simple food for a month. Even a meal in a posh restaurant could be quite cheap, as I and my American friend had found out when we ate at a well-known Chinese restaurant in Karachi city. This place was supposed to be the meeting place of international spies but we found the place decidedly boring and saw nobody looking remotely like a spy. Some people in the Indian sub-continent have a paranoia about spies - the C.I.A., and all that sort of thing.

    Even at the beach teashop, there was a Pakistani from the plain clothes department of, something or other, who used to buy everyone tea and snacks and ask questions such as, "Are you being sponsored by your government"? We found this particular gentleman very useful as he would allow a certain amount of food to be credited to his bill when he was "off duty" at the weekends. The cafe minder was pleased, of course, as it meant extra trade for him and he was also paid punctually. By chance, our Pakistani "friend" went on leave for a few days, just before the remaining half dozen hippies at the beach departed on the next boat to Bombay. My American friend had received a "windfall" from home and bought boat tickets to Bombay for two others and me. We persuaded the teashop owner that our Pakistani "friend" had authorized a generous amount of credit while he was away, and proceeded to run up a largish bill. We did not, of course tell the teashop man of our imminent departure.

The boat journey on a British company's ship was to last a few clays, and cost one hundred rupees for a ticket, deck class, or the then equivalent of five English pounds. Although it was August and the monsoon season, we had a dry trip, and sleeping on deck proved to be pleasant enough. Going deck class meant that we were served the most revolting, highly spiced, watery dishes in our mess. Some of us tried sneaking into the dining area for cabin class passengers, but were soon spotted and given the boot. This ship had come via Kuwait and made the route a regular run.

A few young travelers had got on at Kuwait and made up the deck class foreign contingent to about a dozen. We were all pretty scruffy and casually dressed by comparison with the standards of the average tourist traveler, but compared with the ship's crewmen we looked like scarecrows or refugees. I had given away my leather shoes and my sandals had broken, so my worldly goods on arrival in Bombay consisted of a pair of trousers, two shirts, some underpants, plus a shoulder bag. The climate of India being what it was, I was never to need much more than this.

In August 1966, ten months after leaving England, I presented myself, barefoot, on disembarkation to the customs men in their sheds at Bombay. One asked me where my luggage was, but seemed unconcerned when I opened my almost empty bag. He simply waved me on. Similarly when I told another official that I did not know how long I would be staying, he just shrugged and put a little entry stamp into my passport. As long as you had a British or similar passport you were in, to stay as long as you liked and to do what you liked. Even the passport was no longer a necessity to some, as I later met one loin cloth clad Englishman who had become fed up with carrying his, and had thrown it into the sea. By the time I met him, he had spent eight years in India and he had built up a reputation as a wise holy man - a sadhu. Incidentally this fellow carried nothing around with him in the way of possessions or money. However he managed marvelously as his devotees, who included a judge and a film star, took care of all the mundane aspects of life for him. He lived a bit like Royalty, with someone to carry the purse:

Bombay was hot and sticky between cool showers - normal monsoon weather. I joined up with a couple of other long haired guys off the boat, and wandered into a park to smoke some churrus. Immediately a, large crowd began to gather to watch us, as if we had just landed from outer space. A policeman came over and told us to move on as we were creating a disturbance, but the crowd told him to move on as they were enjoying their free "traveling show". We were getting a preview of just how interested in us the Indian public were, a first indication of the often incredible hospitality and welcome we were to receive in many parts of India. Bombay, I quickly discovered, was much more than the villages, as there in the city people could be curious spectators, but still regarded hippies as mainly of nuisance value. Once we moved out of the city the general interest shown by locals turned into open minded welcome, with generosity showered on us in a manner surpassing that of any other country I had visited.

I managed to survive nearly a week in Bombay, living mainly in parks and scrounging a meal here and there. It was not the India I wanted to be in, as I found it depressingly Westernised in many respects. It had the hustle and bustle of Western cities, but not the affluence. The cultural and religious heritage of India hardly seemed to permeate into the downtown area in which I found myself. I resolved to resume my travels and see the north of India whilst heading for the then hippy "world capital" of Katmandu in Nepal.

Unfortunately I had met up with the crazy English "Captain" and his even crazier mate, and had allowed them to persuade me to join them on the train to Delhi. They had turned up on another boat and were in fine mettle as they told me that not only was ticket less travel acceptable in India, but we could go first class. Then in India, lots of people, including poor foreigners, traveled ticket less. However, they always crammed into the grubby third class carriages that had wooden seats and revolting toilets. I decided to go on the same train as the two eccentrics but instead of joining them in first class, got into "third" with two other fellows off the boat.

    We traveled slowly through the evening and night making great friends with other passengers (and ticket collectors) who were keen to hear our stories. At a station in Rajastan State the next morning, I got off onto the platform to stretch my legs after an uncomfortable night on the boards of the upper tier seats - which were more like baggage racks. I had been lucky to lie down because many had spent the night squashed upright in the congested carriage. Thus feeling still fatigued, I bumped into my English zany friends, who told me that they were having a lovely time in first class, and that I should come and join them.

    Soon I was ensconced with them on the comfortable padded seat of an empty "first" compartment. Almost immediately, before I had time to relax, a ticket collector came round. This fellow instantly took offence to our ticket less presence and ordered us to change to third class at the next station. However, the "Captain" complained that we were first class citizens, not third, and his friend started to chime in with a story about losing our tickets. As we pulled into a small station, seemingly in the middle of nowhere, the ticket collector marched away angrily and returned very quickly with a policeman. The latter began to brandish his handcuffs, and trooped us off to the stationmaster's office. Here we were held while the stationmaster went to check about our "lost" tickets, which, according to my two friends' story, were left in the restaurant of a previous station stop. The policeman seemed to have rejoined the train and for the time being, we were left alone in the small room. There was a door at the rear, which was not only found to be open, but also led to the station forecourt. Here a bus, full of passengers off the train, was revving its engine. We just walked out and hopped on, and were whisked away to a dusty town. Nobody followed, although we spent the night at our first stop, so I guess the railway staff were glad to be rid of us.

The town was in the middle of an area in the grip of famine, as the monsoon had failed. There did not seem to be any food to buy, even in the teashops and cafes, but we ended up as guests in a large house where we were fed bowls of sweet rice pudding. This was my favorite meal at the time, as I still found Indian curries unpalatable. The two Englishmen had decided to get back on the train at the next station and resume their first class journey to Delhi. They seemed totally incorrigible and undeterred by our experience. I had had enough of their maniacal ways and said goodbye, having decided to hitch hike to Delhi.

I made slow progress, getting a variety of truck lifts mainly from Sikh drivers. I was surprised at the number of people I met who could speak reasonable English. The legacy of the British Raj in India is a widespread knowledge of English, with usage of many words, customs and bureaucratic systems - especially in railways, communications and education. This influence is changing though with the passage of time. When Indian people found out that I was English, they would often criticize the state of their country, and tell me how much better things were run in the "good old days" of the British Raj. Some of the older folk remembered the British officials of their area, and would invariably be full of praise for their virtues. I know that Indians would not want British rule again, but their politeness, culture and hospitality made them very courteous with regard to my feelings and background.

Some of the people I met later, who praised the British, had prominent pictures of the Indian "hero", Subash Chandra Bose, in their houses. He was the organizer of the Indian army that fought with the Japanese in Burma against the Allies.

Passing Ajmer and Jaipur, I felt little inclined to stop and admire the marvelous architectural beauty, as I was more concerned with the problems of lifts, food and shelter. I managed to reach Delhi quite easily thanks to the hospitality of the drivers who gave me lifts. Acting on the advice of one Sikh, I headed for a Sikh temple where they had some guest rooms. I had been told that many Hindu and Sikh temples were also ashrams, spiritual centers where any visitor could stay a few days and receive simple food and accommodation free. I "checked in" at the Sikh temple and found a couple of young foreigners staying there in comfort. There seemed to be no attempt at religious indoctrination and as long as you stayed only a few days, you were welcome without strings. I found that if one wanted to stay in any ashram longer, it was generally easy. As long as you did not use drugs or alcohol and attended the *pujas*, or temple services, daily, you could probably make the place your home. Ashram food was vegetarian and basic, and usually you were not allowed to smoke, or do anything that was considered "naughty" by religious standards. I quickly realized why millions in India chose to become sadhus or live as permanent ashram dwellers.

    I learnt that ashrams and Hindu spiritual refuges of all sizes and sectarian types were dotted in their hundreds of thousands all over India. Temples themselves often provided refuge space and food arrangements for wandering mendicants, not to mention the multitude of households that considered it their duty and honor to look after holy men. Small wonder that increasing numbers of travelers from the sixties to the seventies made India their home for a longer time than they had intended. In the seventies, many thousands were to arrive and become *chela*, (disciples), sadhus *and* ashram inmates. There were some hippies who kept their own ideologies and lifestyle and settled down to life in Katmandu or on the beach in Goa, and who remain there to this day. Mother India lived up to her name by providing the necessities of life for those who landed on her doorstep.

I was on the brink of getting ""lost" myself into the folds of India and, especially, Hindu life. Although staying at that time in Delhi and having plans to reach Katmandu, I had also decided that I would visit the holy centers of Hinduism at Rishikesh and Haridwar on the river Ganges. Already I was becoming interested in the world of gurus and holy - men, and wanted to learn something about yoga and meditation. I did not know it at the time, but this awakening interest would divert me from Nepal and lead to a lengthy sojourn in India, I would cease being an English hippy of Christian parentage and become instead a devoted Hindu *sadhak,* spiritual practitioner, *chela,* and sadhu. My years of meat eating would be replaced by a totally vegetarian diet, and I would eschew alcohol and drugs completely. The whole changeover would feel as if it was the most natural thing in the world that could happen to me.

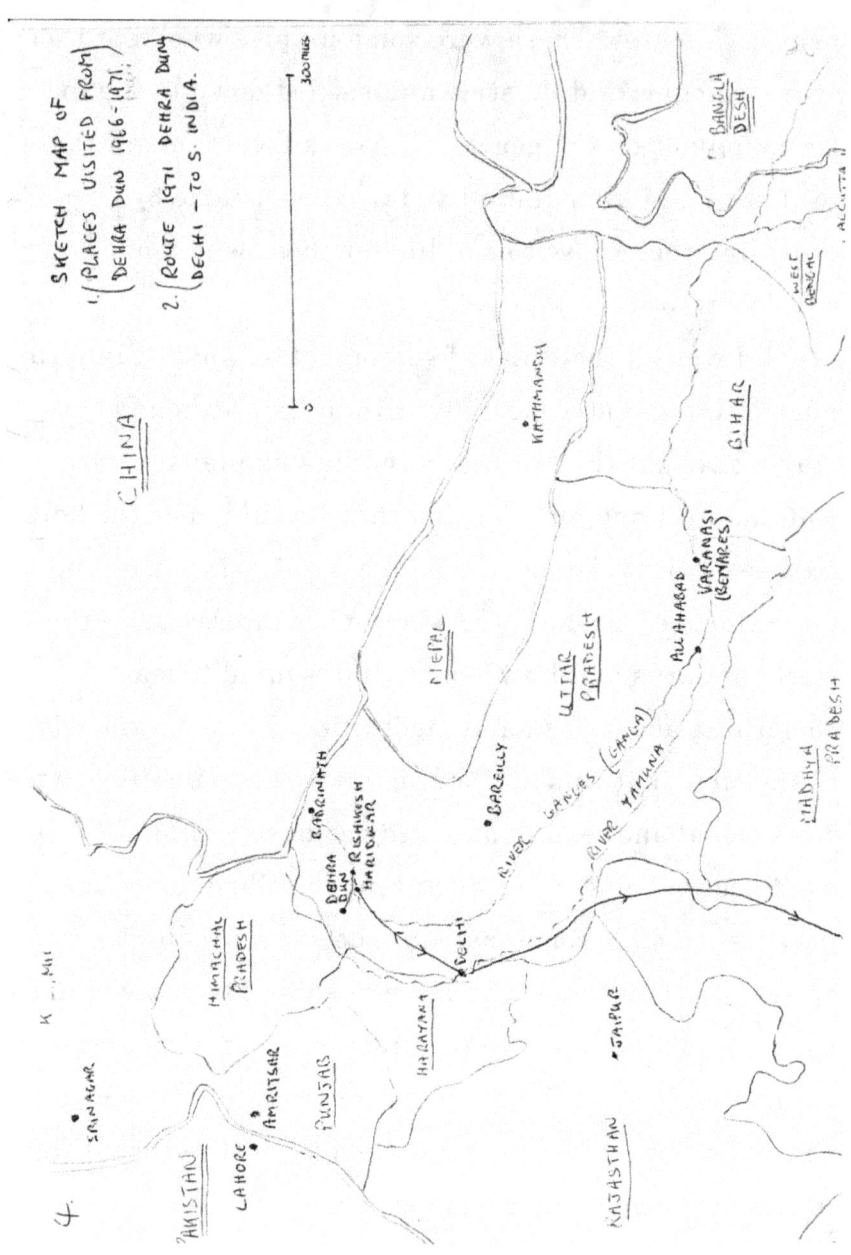

CHAPTER FOUR
Holy Land

I left the Sikh ashram on foot, as I intended to walk to the outskirts of Delhi and try for a lift northwards to the holy town of Haridwar. I spent most of my day wending my way out of the suburbs and by afternoon I felt hot, tired and hungry. 1 found a park like place on the northern outskirts and wandered in for a rest in the shade. It turned out that the park was a Hindu cremation ground and was occupied by a couple of sadhus who had thatch huts. Cremation grounds in India are the favored residence of the ganja, smoking, ash-smeared, half-naked type of holy man. (Ganja is tobacco made from dried cannabis plant).

One of the sadhus waved, beckoning me to sit down beside a smoldering outdoor log fire. This fire was their most important ritual, and they kept it burning, even in summer. As well as having a religious significance, the fire was necessary for brewing the constant tea supply, and for lighting the sacred *chillum,* (straight pipe).

These sadhus spent their time smoking, drinking tea, and chatting with the numerous devotees who squatted around the fire, soaking up the atmosphere. A lot of people seemed to visit these sadhus because it relieved some of the drabness of their own difficult and seemingly inconsequential lives. In India, where earning enough even to avoid starvation is often difficult, holy men of all sorts are seen to be in possession of a glamorous occupation. They are free to wander, obtain food easily and receive much respect. Therefore a householder who is caught in the drudgery of survival will visit the ashram or the sadhu's hut to savor the atmosphere of peace and relaxation that one finds in such places. Devotees will give money and food to an ashram and this will be used partially to feed visitors who stay for a meal. Also any accommodation will have been built by contributions. The true *mahatma,* (great soul), is not supposed to reap much personal gain from all such donations as they are meant, by tradition, to be ploughed back into enlarging the ashram and into providing food and accommodation for visitors and wandering mendicants.

The cremation ground ashram was at the bottom end of the ladder in the Hindu monastic scale. The ash smeared, matted haired resident sadhus were not educated or erudite in scriptural knowledge, and their following was mainly from the working class and castes of Hindus. Most of their devotees would visit them to obtain some charm or talisman to ward off evil spirits and bring prosperity. Since the half-naked or naked sadhu's lived in cremation grounds, they were supposed to have control or power over the dark side of nature, the ghosts and spirits known as *bhutas* and *pretas*.

Although judged as occupying a low position in the hierarchy of Hindu holy men, the ganja smoking sadhu's are part of the same system that functions in the huge, multi storied ashrams of powerful renunciate monk *sannyasins*.

The well-known Indian gurus with their hordes of Western disciples have their roots in this system, although many have left it far behind. In India, the word sadhu, (meaning "one who does good"), is applied to the whole range of do-gooders, whether they live in the cremation grounds with their fires, or whether they run large spiritual centers.

From the cremation ground I moved to a nearby village to stay with a family. I had been invited by one of the visitors to the cremation ground to go to his house for a meal and I ended up staying a week. I got my first real contact with everyday Hindu culture and society there, as I was introduced to nearly every family in the main street. I also met a shaven headed, orange robed sannyasin. I found that within this particular order of sadhus, there was a wide variety of types from the austere, wandering mendicant to the important, erudite head of a sect. The "top dogs" amongst the sannyasins had influence that was sometimes stronger than say that of Christian bishops, and even at the lower end of the scale, much respect was accorded to the "cloth". Their title was always *Swamiji,* (which is similar to Reverend). However, the word swami is also used to talk about sannyasins in general.

The sannyasin that I had met had come to stay in the same house as me, and I managed to learn quite a lot about his lifestyle, which apparently was fairly average for many thousands like him. He belonged to the holy orders following the Vedanta tradition and believed in the teachings of the Hindu scriptures from the post Vedic period. These scriptures, such as the Upanishads and some commentaries on the Bhagavat Gita, teach that the world is unreal, that the individual soul is no different from the cosmic soul, and that the way to self-realization or liberation lies through renunciation. The sannyasin whom I met seemed to live a fairly austere life in that he refrained from intoxicants, sex, and "luxuries", such as sleeping on a mattress. However, he did well wherever he went as he was fed vegetarian delicacies at the houses in which he stayed) and he received much respect, as people would bow down and touch his feet. Furthermore, I noticed that visitors who came to the house for *darshan,* (holy visit), used to place plenty of rupee notes at his feet.

The holy men in India come in many different forms, and hold a variety of beliefs under the Hindu umbrella of philosophies and religious sects. They are all well respected by a large proportion of the population, and receive a variety of benefits ranging from the base essentials to gifts of a fortune. They are free to set up their home anywhere - including in recent times Switzerland and California. The principle in Hindu culture by which they are supposed to function is based on service in kind by the devotees, with reciprocation in the way of spiritual teachings and blessings by the holy men. For the ochre robed sannyasins, there is a huge system of ashrams around the country, where several hundred of sadhus can live without begging or without having to ask for anything. These ashrams are not the same as the monasteries of the Christian world, although there are similarities. They have their "Chiefs and Indians", with the top places being passed along from a head monk to a selected disciple. They have a lot of independence, in administrative terms, from each other because of the wide range of worship that they encompass. Whereas many Hindus will worship all the gods (known as *devas*), most usually have allegiance to a particular favorite - the *Ishta Deva*. One person concentrates on the incarnations of *Vishnu* and is a *Vaishnavite*, worshipping *Rama or Krishna*. Another is a *Shaivite* and follows *Shiva,* the god whose phallus shaped, stone symbol, the lingam, is found in thousands of

Indian temples. Yet another worships *Shakti,* the female power or divinity embodied in the deities of *Kali, Durga, and Parvati.*

Although many sannyasins are *Vedantis* and worship the formless soul, nearly all of them worship the gods and goddesses. For the majority, Shiva is the favored deity. Vedantis believe in a formless Absolute which is *Sat-Chit-Ananda,* (Existence-Knowledge-Bliss). However, nearly all the ashrams or *muttams* have temples devoted to one or more of the Hindu pantheon. If they do not have a deity's image or idol in their temples, they will often have a marble statue of their deceased guru, and worship that. They explain this contradiction of philosophy by saying that the practice of meditation on the formless inner self goes hand in hand with the outward worship of deities and gurus. The outer worship purifies the mind and makes possible the difficult achievement of inward concentration. Vedanta is a theoretical philosophy only and not a pathway in itself, for those who worship external deities.

Staying in the village near Delhi, I began to learn and appreciate something of the vastness and complexity of Hindu religion and culture. I really plunged in at the deep end when I arrived in one of India's holiest towns - Haridwar at the foot of the Himalayas and on the Ganges. I was taken there by a sadhu who had matted locks and an ash smeared body. I met him in the village as he used to frequent the tea and sweet shop of my hosts. We got on a train to do the two hundred mile journey and arrived without problems at Haridwar station; gateway to the Himalayan route that led to the source of the Ganges. In India many people will add honorific suffixes when referring to rivers such as the Ganges or Narmada. Thus Ganga (Ganges) becomes Gangaji. "Ji' is an honorific usually added to any respected person or place's name in polite speech. Mataji and Pitaji are the correct terms of address for mother and father and thus sadhuji, or swamiji, or perhaps maharaji, which means literally "great king". Babaji is another common term of respect for a wise person. However, the word baba also means young child or innocent one.

Haridwar is connected with Rishikesh, a few miles upstream. This is the place that gained some international recognition when the Beatles went there to see Mahesh Yogi the founder of the Transcendental Meditation (T.M.) groups around the world. Both Haridwar and Rishikesh are crowded with temples, ashrams and muttams of all shapes, sizes, and followings. The area teems with sannyasins, sadhus, pilgrims and devotees. Many people pass through here on their way north to Badrinath and Kedarnath – both major pilgrimage centers deep in the Himalaya. The route northwards to the source of the Ganges used to be by foot only from Rishikesh, but now buses ply in their dozens on the road developed by the military. It is, of course, a politically sensitive area for the Indian government, and foreigners wishing to go beyond Rishikesh and into the mountains used to need a special permit.

Many pilgrims come to the Ganges at Rishikesh and Haridwar because a dip in her waters here is considered more auspicious than in some other parts. Then again at certain days of the year a sacred bath at Haridwar accrues even more holy benefits. On such days, several hundred thousand pilgrims can jam into a special area at Haridwar for their dip. Usually a few people get squashed or drown on these occasions, and now and then there is some mass panic and several get killed.

Even worse in this respect are the Kumbha Melas: fairs for pilgrims and holy men, held on certain days of particular years at the confluence of the Ganges and Jamuna rivers at Allahabad. Then the crowds go into astronomical figures and when, as in one year, there is a mass stampede, the death toll is bad. Hindus go to places like Varanasi, which was Benaras, specifically to die there, and dying in any holy center is believed to accrue great merit. That is why the crowds continue to jam like lemmings into small spaces by rivers, or in temples, on auspicious days - whatever the risk. Cholera and other problems are perhaps an even bigger worry for the authorities that have to control huge religious gatherings. Epidemics can spring up overnight and kill hundreds in a day.

My sadhu friend who took me to Haridwar was very much an outdoor type, and he led me to meet his mates who lived under trees by the banks of the Ganges. They were very nice to me, feeding me on *laddhus*, which are sweets made of wheat cooked with much clarified butter, (ghee), and sugar. Another delicacy that I tried became my favorite; this being a sweet made from milk which had been boiled down slowly in an open, wok like pan. The milk solids were mixed with sugar and the sweet, called *burfi*, is then cut into squares, and decorated with edible silver paper.

The open air sadhus also taught me how to hold a chillum. The chillum is a straight earthen ware pipe, with a small round orifice at the bottom and a one-inch diameter tapered bowl at the top. It is usually six inches or so in length, although larger specimens are used on ceremonial occasions. I have seen one in use that was two foot long, which held a wad of ganja the size of a fist! The chillum is lit with a glowing ember made from a knot of rope dipped in the log fire that burns continually. The hot ember is pulled out of the fire with tongs and placed on top of the chillum, which would have been filled with ganja tobacco. The sadhus then pass the pipe around, each using a square of damp muslin cloth to grip the pipe and filter the smoke. The chillum is smoked by sadhus only after chanting incantations to the god Shiva. The correct procedure is to grip the pipe in the palm of one's hand and lay the other on top, leaving a gap between the thumb and first finger. Then, after exhaling, one sucks deeply on the gap in the cupped hands, drawing the smoke deeply into the lungs. If one is any good at it, flames should shoot from the top of the chillum, and the sadhus will nod appreciatively. (Now you know the correct etiquette if you find yourself seated around the fire of an ash smeared *fakir*, on the banks of the Ganges)

The chillums I smoked in Haridwar were to be my last, except for a few polite "puffs" on rare occasions later. I gave up smoking completely within a week of that time and stayed a nonsmoker until I returned to a Westernized lifestyle ten years later, when I took to smoking tobacco briefly. It was the last time I was ever a drug user, and was also the beginning of a period of ten years of strict vegetarianism, during which I never even had an egg. The food I had been receiving in India was vegetarian and that was all that would be available to me in the future. I took to my new diet easily and began to enjoy the simple Hindu food, although I remained as skinny as a rake during all my stay in India. Even though

I tried to put on weight on occasions. I think that the general low fat levels of my food and the withering effect of the hot climate kept me at a steady 60 kilos, or 125 lbs.

My next stop was Rishikesh and the well-known Shivananda Ashram. As this was the home of serious minded swamis and their largely Western devotees, my sadhu friend said goodbye to me. He had no place amongst the cultured practitioners, who, with stern attitude, sought to purify and awaken their souls. This was not the environment for the ash smeared fakir who enjoyed a good "smoke".

Swami Shivananda who set up this ashram had become well known in India and overseas, mainly through his prolific publications, which were all available in English. He had died some years before I reached his ashram - or rather he had "left his mortal coil", as English speaking Indians like to term it. In this place a few dozen Western disciples resided. English was used by foreigner and Indian alike, and there was strict adherence to a daily programme of yoga, *asanas* (postures), meditation, and scriptural study. A world apart from the log fires of naked ascetics who lived under trees:

I was given a room without furniture except a string bed, and provision was made for meals to be brought to me.

Like the middle-aged ladies and gents who had arrived by plane, from, typically, America, Germany and Britain, I was expected to participate in the programme. Indeed I attended the early morning yoga exercise classes and meditated in the shrine of Swami Shivananda.

The shrine of a holy saint in India is called a *samadhi*, a word synonymous with the state of trance obtained in meditation. Most Hindus are cremated, but the self-realized souls, the yogis and gurus, are often buried, with their bodies placed in the lotus posture. Some sages in India have actually chosen their date of death, and have died whilst in trance, seated in the lotus posture. Others have been placed like this by their devotees and disciples. The burial takes place with .much religious fervor.

The corpse of the holy man is lowered with chanting and ritual ceremony in front of an often sizeable crowd. Then a shrine is built around the site, with the well-known gurus getting a marble statue and opulent temple surroundings. It is thus a, Hindu temple with just the same degree of *puja* or ritual performed there as in any temple of Shiva or Krishna. I had learnt to fold my palms in supplication when entering temples. As well as this, I knew that one was supposed to have had a bath and put on clean clothing before entering such places. I quite happily went along with all of this ceremony as I found Hindu ritualistic practices quite interesting. However, I did not believe that much spiritual benefit could be gained by following the Hindu rules and regulations. My interest was mainly in meditation. I wanted to know all about the means whereby one was supposed to achieve nirvana or *moksha,* (freedom from the cycle of births and earthly suffering).

When I began to look for a guru who could guide me in the spiritual path to self-realization, I realized that I had arrived in the right country. I had travelled a long time not knowing what I was looking for. Now I felt that all my travels and wanderings would be useless if I did not stop and work towards achieving a degree of inner awareness or self-knowledge. I was quite prepared then to give up or change anything of my lifestyle or personality in order to attain what I felt I needed. I was ready to embark on a course of rigorous self-discipline if necessary. I wanted, more than I had ever wanted in my life, to achieve a level of deep spiritual insight - to become a yogi with mental and physical control over my life.

My first effort at finding a guru was a nonevent. I had heard of the Maharishi, ("great sage"), Mahesh Yogi who lived on the opposite bank of the Ganges from Rishikesh. He had built an ashram of twenty or so rooms and was catering largely for foreigners. I think this was around the time the Beatles became interested in him and but before his "career" really took off in the West. I found the place empty and dull, as the man himself was not in residence, and there seemed to be nobody else there except for a manager and a few servants. However, I was given a room and stayed a few days. On my departure I was given a bill, just like in a hotel. This was the only time I ever got a bill from an ashram during all my ten years in India. It was one of the few times I was to experience a truly westernized ashram, with a price for everything. This is the same today with the Maharishi's brainchild (T.M. or Transcendental Meditation), as it is now with many "Eastern' spiritual organizations. One pays, then one is taught. This system is in contrast to the Hindu tradition of free provision of spiritual facilities, with the emphasis on totally unsolicited gifts from the disciples.

The traditional Hindu devotee serves the guru by work or by donation according to means and wishes, and the guru reciprocates in spiritual kind. It is not a bazaar transaction where the goods have a price tag.
The influx of non-Indian disciples and devotees into ashrams changed the system for gurus, many whom have now traveled out of India. They now charge for lectures and their "blessings", in India and elsewhere.

In the Hindu view, to be a guru means to be above all attachment to worldly goods (including money) and certainly not to seek to make a nice profit. Incidentally, I could not pay my bill at the Maharishi's center, and they seemed shocked at meeting a foreigner without cash in his pocket. However, I was allowed to go on my way without hassle, musing that that particular place certainly would not be able to cater for any Indian at that time, except the wealthy.

Since arriving in Rishikesh I had begun to sit in meditation and do yoga exercises early each morning and at sunset. I was finding it difficult to concentrate either because of mosquitoes or because of my own fidgeting. To sit even cross legged then was painful after about ten minutes. I despaired of achieving anything like the six hours daily that yogis were supposed to spend in the lotus posture. I thought that if I moved into the foothills of the Himalayas, I would be able to escape some of the heat and perhaps be able to concentrate better.

I decided to head towards Mussori, which is a hill station situated above the plains and the town of Dehra Dun. The large town of Dehra Dun itself was a few hours journey from Rishikesh, and I managed to get a lift during a late monsoon storm, arriving in the town just as the rain stopped. I had decided to visit an ashram that was situated on the outskirts of town in the area called Race Course Road, near the police training ground. I heard of this ashram from some Americans staying in Rishikesh, who had told me that the swami who lived there spoke excellent English and had a European disciple.

As I wandered into the area of Race Course Road, I found myself at the edge of a large expanse of flat common land. A road ran around the area which, logically enough, had been used in the time of British rule as a place to race horses. On the furthest edge of the flat land, some half a mile from the nearest house, was a walled enclosure containing the gardens, orchard and buildings of Shri Swargapuri Ashram. A large signboard, in Hindi and English, advertised this place named "heaven town", (S*warg & Puri*). The word Shri is attached to Hindu names, (either persons or places), as respectful prefix. Underneath the large lettering for the ashram's name, there was a very long title which seemed to be the name of the resident guru, Shri 108 Swami Chaitanya Prakash Ananda Tirth Maharaj, M.A. Vedanta Archarya, (plus a few more qualifications). That was indeed his name (and titles), which on explanation becomes a little less complicated than it seemed. Shri and swami have already been explained. *Chaitanya* means life spirit or consciousness, *prakash* means light, and *ananda*, (meaning bliss), is the usual suffix after sannyasins' names. Tirth means place of pilgrimage, and is one of ten such "surnames" pertaining to different branches of sannyasins. Two other such "surnames" are *puri,* (town or dwelling), and *giri* (mountain). The use of the number 108 in a title is an embellishment, referring to the one hundred and eight *rishis* (sages) that have given their names and souls to an equal number of stars in the sky.

The whole business of names of holy men is complicated by the use of other honorific titles bestowed on them by their followers and devotees, or even adopted by the swami or sadhu himself. These forms of address include *maharishi* (great sage), *bhagavan* (lord.), and *paramhamsa* (great swan). A Paramhansa is a sage who is able to float on the pool of worldly desires and temptations without sinking. Or, like the mythological swan who separates milk from water, a sage who can separate the good essence of life from the dross. All the titles employed by Hindu custom in common use have become somewhat debased, like some words used in advertising, such as fantastic, amazing, stupendous, and so on.

However, qualifications in age old subjects such as Sanskrit, Vedanta and *shastras* (scriptures), are usually obtained only after years of intensive study, in some cases, ten years, for a Sanskrit "degree". Swamis who have various indigenous qualifications have often gained their letters whilst living as *brahmacharis,* (celibate students), before becoming sannyasins. According to ancient tradition the first phase of Hindu life is that of the celibate student (brahmacharya), followed by that of householder (*grihastha*). The next stage is that of the hut dwelling hermit (*varnaprastha*), who lives on roots and fruits in the forest. This hermit stage was supposed to precede the renunciation of all possessions and abodes, and the adoption of sannyas. However, sannyasins today tend to live in or own ashrams. Also in current times sannyas can be is taken up at any stage of life, prior to, or after some period of married life. Technically speaking, many of India's sannyasins have actually adopted the stage, of varnaprastha.

CHAPTER FIVE
Guru Found

When I walked into the ashram I found that there was some sort of lecture going on in a large verandah. A corpulent swami in bright orange robes was sitting cross legged on a platform of wood that was the size and shape of a bed. The platform was covered in bright orange cloth and the swami sat on a deerskin in front of a small reading table. He was reading from a large volume of some scriptural work, whilst an audience of devotees sat on the floor on either side of the platform. Four male listeners sat on one side of the verandah, whilst several dozen women were spread out on the other side.

    I stood outside on the lawn for a minute until the swami invited me to step inside and sit down. I sat on the edge of his platform, an act which horrified the audience, as only holy men of equal standing to the swami were supposed to do that sort of thing. The fact that I had committed an extremely irreverent act did not register with me at that time of course. One of the male devotees quickly ushered me to a place on the carpeted floor, where

    I sat uncomfortably whilst the scripture reading and discourse continued. It became apparent to me that the swami was held in awe by his audience because, at the close of the "sermon", they all queued up to prostrate before him, touching his feet before departing.

After nearly all the devotees had gone, the swami began to speak to me in very good English. He said that a couple of young Englishmen had recently stayed for a few months at the ashram, and had become disciples of his. He asked me then if I wished to stay for a few days, or months, or even years. I explained that I was interested in finding a guru who could teach me yoga and meditation, but that I did not have all that much interest in Hindu ritualism.

He replied that my chosen methods were indeed a way of attaining samadhi, or union with divine consciousness. However, he said that I needed to learn about the other "paths" of *bhakti yoga,* (devotional observances), and *karma yoga* (selfless service). He said for most people a combination of methods was the only successful way. He also pointed out that to get anywhere in sadhana one needed the guidance of a Sat, or True, Guru - a self-realized soul who could trigger the necessary changes. Swami Chaitanya Prakash Ananda did not hesitate to tell me that he had a double M.A. in Sanskrit and Philosophy as well as a host of scriptural qualifications from the Hindu University in Varanasi.

I was quite impressed by this swami, as he seemed to have the right qualifications and knowledge of every aspect of Hinduism, combined with a good degree of Western education.

He did, seem to be a very orthodox sannyasin who followed scriptural rules, but nevertheless I thought that he could have the key to the spiritual knowledge that I sought. I decided there and then to stay and become a disciple, for a while at least! Quite soon I decided to go along with the Hindu ritualism for the sake of learning about yoga and meditation.

I was given a small hut in which to live. It was a tin roofed, brick building situated in a corner of the ashram's garden of an acre or so. I had a charpoy, mattress and blanket, plus a *lota* (water pot) and a steel plate for food. As it was excruciatingly hot under the tin roof, I took to spending a lot of my time on the verandah, attached to which were swamiji's comfortable rooms and kitchen. The food I received was very simple and consisted of a main meal at midday of *rotis*, dhal and vegetables; with a snack in the evening of rice and lentils cooled together or re heated leftovers.

I also received a metal glass full of tea in the morning and afternoon. The kitchen was run by some of the female devotees who came to listen to the daily satsang or spiritual discourse, staying on to cook meals and clean around the place. Swamiji's meals seemed to be quite elaborate affairs and needed a good supply of helpers, while any other ashram residents got basic fare.

There was only one other disciple living in the place at the time. He was a young India who was a bramachari. He was studying at Varanasi, but in between terms lived as swamiji's chela and helped out in the ashram's three temples.

I found that swamiji lived in a fairly affluent style and that this was the norm for sadhus of any public standing in India. The monk's life of austere simplicity, wandering with begging bowl in hand was practiced by choice by few sadhus. Those that did live by begging were accorded little status by the Hindu public. The holy men who were erudite and gave lecture tours or yoga classes pulled in the disciples, the accolades and the money. Status hunting between sannyasins led to rivalry and competition to see who could attract the largest, (and wealthiest), following. Brilliant discourses, advanced scriptural knowledge, or displays of yogic skills were the means to bring in the donations that built the luxurious abodes of "top" swamis. Once a well-appointed ashram had been constructed, public acknowledgement and acclaim followed, and more devotees could be attracted by a snowball effect.

Status and position seeking in the hierarchy of sadhus often led to bickering over trivial matters. Later in India when I attended large religious conferences, I was to see a lot of competition amongst the learned holy men who gathered to give public lectures. There would be a large platform of several tiers on which were placed cushions and rugs for the speakers to sit on. With up to thirty sadhus and swamis on stage, one could guarantee plenty of intensive rivalry over the question of who should sit on the higher levels. With a crowd of up to ten thousand in front, the matter of who was seen to be the most important person was of great significance to these "saints", who had supposedly renounced the afflictions of the material world.

A few days after arriving at the ashram, I was given some white cotton cloth to wear instead of my tatty trousers and shirt. This cloth was in two metre lengths, which I simply wrapped around my waist to form a dhoti or draped around my shoulders to form my shawl, (or *chaddar*). For underwear I was given some strips of cloth to make a *langoti*. One strip was tied around my waist and the other, wider, piece I passed round the front of the waistband, between my legs, and tied it at the back of the waistband.

Thus I was outfitted with the standard basic kit of all sadhus, albeit in the white color used by brahmacharis and not the orange of sannyasins.

In India people take baths frequently, and simple cloths such as dhotis are very handy as they can be wrung dry and simply spread on some grass or a bush. They will dry in ten minutes even under a winter sun, and so a sadhu can always wear a fresh cloth after a bath. Both a bath and fresh clothing are considered essential by Hindus before one is purified sufficiently to be able to enter a temple or perform puja. Often

Brahmins (priestly caste) and sadhus will take a quick bath and change their dhotis after going to the toilet.

A bath in India does not mean sitting in a tub. That is considered very impure or unclean. One either has to sit under a running tap or use a bucket of water, scooping with a cup. A wooden board is often used for squatting on whilst bathing, and some clothes are left on as nudity is definitely taboo, even in the bathroom. Women also bathe this way, leaving on their sari which is dexterously unwrapped wet whilst a fresh one is wound on.

In cold weather, warm water is often used, but generally in India's heat one wants to take only refreshing cold dips as often as possible. Incidentally, a person taking a ritual bath in sacred waters such as the Ganges is supposed to have a wash at home first, in order to accrue the full merit. It is perhaps interesting to note that gallons of untreated sewage are poured daily into the Ganges where it runs through towns and cities:

In the Dehra Dun ashram, the day began at about 4 a.m., which was the time to get up and go off to the fields for toilet purposes. This meant a walk of some distance in order to get clear of the houses and onto wasteland. Now here is one aspect of Indian life that I found utterly awkward, annoying and unhygienic. To the Indian, a good bowel movement at a regular time in the early morning is an essential of life.

Fair enough! However it is more than that. It is an obsession for many, and at least an important topic for most.

That is still, I think, a reasonable outlook. What is baffling, though is that given the importance of the bowel's functions, there are often no facilities provided to make this process an easy one.

Few Indians possessed a toilet where I lived and traveled. Those that are available were often nauseating. Many villagers and town dwellers used a spot outside the limit of the houses, often to the side of entrance paths. Hence the need for a good bowel movement first thing in the morning because it is still dark and some privacy is possible.

However, in a medium sized village, if you go out just before daybreak, you will be participating in a mini human traffic jam. The result of this daily migration is a smelly, offensive mess that rings habitable areas. It is true that the heat of the sun quickly breaks down human excrement, but often when approaching a village by pathways from the fields, one is assailed by a horrible smell. If I was walking to a new village that I had not visited before, I knew when I was nearly there. An awful odor is the sign that you have reached the outskirts.

The smelly destruction of country walking areas, plus the terrible inconvenience of day time bowel needs, was one of the reasons why I could never totally accept the simple Indian village life. Even when toilets were available, they were often so distasteful that a trek to the nearest ravine or gully was preferable.

The ashram at Dehra Dun was no exception to the usual predicament, and the need to defecate meant a quarter mile walk to the nearest scrub land. At least there was an area available away from heavy population, with some degree of privacy. Later at the ashram some reasonable toilets were built, and I am happy to say that during my years in India the general situation did seem to be undergoing improvement.

Of course, in the middle of big towns and cities, most, but not all, people had to use some kind of indoor toilet. This was often a hole in the ground leading down into some sort of receptacle. This gathering pot was cleaned out daily by a human being of the *bhangi* caste. This caste was considered "untouchable"' even by other low caste people and I could understand why. When I saw them carrying their buckets of filth balanced on their heads I was shocked by their appearance and, quite naturally, wanted to jump out of their way. However, I was even more disturbed by thoughts about their quality of life, or rather lack of it.

I started getting up early and going off into the bush before my bath, as is customary. However the walk was mostly a waste of time as I found my bowels did not want to work when I wanted then to. Consequently I had to troop off again during the day, which was all right some of the time. The problem was that my stomach found the complete conversion to ashram diet a difficult task, and the ensuing diarrhea problems were an incredible nuisance.

After my early awakening under a garden tap, I headed off to the ashram verandah for a meditation session. I did not find it too difficult getting up so early as it was customary for me to go to sleep early, and have a sometimes have a nap in the heat of the day. For most of the year, the early hours of the day were the only bearable ones. After ten o'clock, or earlier in summer, it was best not to venture out into the heat and walk unless necessary.

When I first started to meditate, I found the whole experience very painful, mainly on account of the difficulty I felt sitting cross legged for any length of time. After sitting still for about five minutes my legs would begin firstly to ache mildly and then to send out signals of great pain. I felt that I had to sit as still as a rock to meditate and I found my lack of body flexibility very frustrating. I took to practicing yoga asanas, (postures) twice daily and began to achieve a degree of suppleness in my limbs.

It took me a few months before I could sit for half an hour in reasonable comfort, but much longer to achieve the lotus posture for even a short time. The lotus posture or *padmasana* is the recommended pose for all serious yogis as it makes possible an upright and straight spinal rigidity, which in turn helps the mind to be freed from bodily distractions. It took me about a year to achieve a comfortable padmasana, and several years before I could sit still for three hours at a stretch.

Traditionally Indians have always sat on the floor in their houses and shops, although a raised flat platform is often used. A mattress like base with a bolster to lean on is the common provision in many places. More houses were getting chairs or a sofa, and these are more often used when visitors arrive. Even so, the women did not get to sit in chairs as much as the men, firstly because they often spend most of the time in the kitchen, and secondly was not the done thing according to their role in society. The fact that women have better health by avoiding chairs could be thought of as poor recompense for their inferior social position in orthodox households.

However, few women in seemed to complain about their role, perhaps because so many were brought up in without getting the chance to think about their place in life. This can be said equally of the men, who were not encouraged not to question the rules that have been laid down by tradition over the centuries. There is, of course, in India a custom of superior to inferior role relations that goes much deeper than the male to female equation. The whole social stratum was so bound up with casteism and religious precepts that it did make India seem an incredibly unequal society. I think many Indians acknowledged the negative aspects of their complex social structure, &and changes were afoot.

After the difficulty of sitting still to meditate, the next major problem was my mind. Whenever I meditated in the morning, I tended to nod off to sleep, and in the evening session I often felt that I was passing time until supper. Food was assuming greater mental proportions than it had ever done before. I always felt hungry, no matter how many rotis I had eaten. I think that the low fat, high fibre diet that I was getting, plus the yoga exercises I was doing, had stirred up my metabolism. Consequently my appetite was like an all-consuming furnace, and I spent a lot of time dreaming of eating sweets and rich foods. When I did manage to overcome sleepiness and thoughts about food, I often slipped into dreamy states and visualized all sorts of things totally unconnected with my new found spiritual life.

I imagined scenes in which cowboys and Red Indians fought battles similar to ones I had seen in films as a boy. I visualized pubs, musical groups, family scenes and events from the past, often with great vividness and appropriate colors. From talking to swamiji and reading yoga treatises I learnt that this mental activity was quite normal for the beginner, and was a cleansing phenomenon, because the memory facilities were being stimulated, by meditation. When a lot of the mind's subconscious material had been "released", then I found that I could meditate without thoughts and visions from this inner level, unless I chose to focus on something in particular.

I was initiated into two mantras by swamiji. Mantras are words which have a sacred and spiritual significance. I was told that the quickest way to self-realization and mental stillness was by repeating the mantras as frequently as possible until they became automatic. The repetition, or *japa*, would concentrate the mind, diverting it inwards from the outer world. When the mind became free from all thought patterns and only the mantra japa remained, then awareness of the inner peace and bliss would surface, as it were, and replace the different mental moods with an all-enveloping calmness.

Anxious to achieve results as quickly as I could, I began to repeat my sacred words over and over endlessly throughout the day. For the purposes of this japa, I was given some malas, or rosaries of *Tulsi* wood made from the sacred Indian basil plant. For wearing around my neck, I received some knobbly beads from the *Rudraksha* tree that grows in Nepal. Rudraksha means the "protection of Rudra" (Shiva). Almost all malas are made of 108 beads. This is the prescribed holy number pertaining to the 108 rishis (sages) who are represented as 108 stars. I was given one later made of 1008 Tulsi beads, a number again having religious significance.

The Tulsi plant has an especial relevance for worshippers of the various forms of Vishnu, the Vaishnavites. Rudraksha, on the other hand, is worn by the followers of Shiva, including most sannyasins. Tulsi and Rudsaksha are not meant to be worn together, and indeed the two groups of Vaishnavites and Shaivites have a lot of differences between them. In long past times, the two groups led by various kings used to clash, and pitched battles were fought by the armies of those kings of different religious allegiance, even though they were all equally Hindus. Perhaps this is a parallel to the present day conflicts between Protestants and Catholics, or Shia and Sunni Moslems.

Sannyasins, in the majority, seemed to have Shiva as their main deity, although they often worshiped the other gods and goddesses. Some of the white robed sadhus, however, belonged to pure Vaishnavite sects, along with a minority of the ochre robed monks. These sadhus and swamis are generally very strict in their allegiance to Rama or Krishna, and are very restricted regarding which deities they can worship. They often argue vehemently against the philosophy of some Vedantis who believe in the ultimate formlessness and indivisibility of a God - head. Thus the "Hare Krishnas" of Western fame interpret the world as being the Lila (play) of Krishna only, and may disregard other Hindu views.

They may be opposed to the Vedantic idea of the inner soul being the same as the cosmic soul and see themselves as *Bhaktas* (devotees) of Krishna exclusively, and never of an impersonal entity, or even of the deities of Shaivites or Shaktas.

Having been initiated into the mysteries of meditation and yoga, I was given a Hindu name during a special fire ceremony. I gave up not only my English name but also my previous personality for a "true blue" Hindu identity, I became Ram Prakash Brahmachari, the "light of Rama" and thus a chela of my first guru.

Ram (or Rama) is one of the avatars (incarnations) of Vishnu - the god who is portrayed in Hindu mythology as the sustainer and protector of the universe. The story of Rama, the Ramayana, is the most popular and well known of the mythological epics in India. The Mahabharatam, which includes the Bhagavat Gita and the stories about Krishna's life, is the next most popular religious book. Personally, I was not really interested at this time in Ram worship, but that did not matter too much because in ancient Sanskrit the word Ram simply means "fire".

Equipped with all the accoutrements of a serious *sadhaka*, or practitioner on the Hindu path, I began over the next few months to enter into a regular programme of serious meditation, japa, yoga, and study. Any spare time I spent helping in the gardens or in the three ashram temples. A few hours a day were also allocated to listening to swamiji's lectures and discourses in the satsang. (Association or sang, with the wise and truthful, or sat.

At first, attending the public daily talk or sermon given in the Hindi by swamiji, seemed for me rather a waste of time as I could not understand a word. Several devotees who came to the ashram suggested that I get hold of a book and learn some of the language. However at school I had hated grammar and language study in general, and I did not want to do any study in this direction. I was only interested in reading the English books in swamiji's extensive library.

There were plenty of excellent translations on the subjects of yoga, Vedanta, and on general aspects of the Hindu culture and religion. The Vedantic teachings are to be found in the Upanishads, the works written towards the end of the Vedic period. After the Vedic treatises dealing with sacrifices, rituals and pious deeds, the Upanishads went in a dramatically different direction. They dealt with questions of the soul, the universe and the nature of reality. The commentaries that followed were written by learned sages who had become recluses and sannyasins. Shankaracharya of the ninth century was perhaps the most well-known of these commentators.

Even today, much similar work is published in books such as those of the Ramakrishna Mission in Calcutta.

The Vedantin believes that the world is an illusion, like a dream, and gives it the name *Maya*. The reality or truth of life is an all pervading, formless consciousness (Brahma), which is identical to the inner soul or *Atman*. Owing to this Maya, we feel that we, God and the universe are three separate entities. However, when false knowledge or ignorance, (*avidya*), is cut asunder by self-knowledge and introspection, the veil before our minds falls away to reveal our true natures. Most Hindu gurus who follow this basic philosophy preach that self-knowledge, or *Atma Gyana*, cannot be attained without firstly the help of a guru, and secondly the practice of some form of sadhana.

Of course, many spiritual leaders over the centuries have formed their own differing philosophies, and those who refute the "undivided", (or *Advaita*), Vedantic ideas usually believe in some form of a separate God head. Their means of attaining salvation relies heavily on the path of bhahkti devotion, as opposed to that of gyana or (knowledge. However all spiritual leaders in Hinduism stress the need for a guru.

Along with my meditation, japa and studies, (mainly in Vedanta and the Upanishads), I was learning temple lore, and gaining insight into the path of bhakti. I learnt how to clean and prepare the temples and how to offer the flowers, incense and other materials whilst uttering the correct Sanskrit incantations. I began to learn hymns and excerpts from the Bhagavat Gita in relatively simple Sanskrit, (once I had learned to read the *Devanagari* script). The interest in the spiritual language of Hinduism gave me, without studying any grammar, an ever-widening vocabulary of both Sanskrit and Hindi words. Within a year I was able to perform the complete temple service for the three small temples and began to do so on my own, to the astonishment of the local devotees who came to worship.

I had to wash the temple floors, the images, make fresh offerings of flowers and incense, and then make a round of all three temples ringing the bells and waving the oil lamps. People would come from the nearby houses for the *arati* or "lights and bells" finale, which was always accompanied by specified hymns. As I had been accepted as the *Pujari*, (temple priest), I felt quite proud at times to be leading up to a dozen devotees in their daily ritual worship. I never felt that there was anything unusual in being an Englishman in charge of the temple worship. The public who visited never seemed to mind the fact that I was not a Brahmin, or one of the priestly caste. According to Hindu scriptures, a foreigner from "over the seas" is a *mlecha* or outcaste.

However, Hindu religion on the whole is very adaptable as it is an amalgam of an endless range of philosophies, practices and cultures. One thing I knew for sure was that the atmosphere and aura around the daily pujas and aratis was one of exuberance and gaiety, a long way from the sombre Christian church ceremonies I remembered from childhood. I enjoyed messing around in the temples - something that I had never experienced in England whilst in church services.

In my studies of the Hindu culture I became intrigued by the complexities and diversities of its past and present growth. To me, the most baffling aspect was, and still is, the combination of Vedic ritual, image or deity worship and the Advaita Vedanta and Yoga philosophies. All these major aspects contradict each other in many ways, sometimes going in totally opposite directions.

The Vedic culture is supposedly "imported" by early Aryan invaders from the direction of Persia and southern Russia, centuries before the birth of Christ. It contains the practices and beliefs of a community, which lived a nomadic existence, dependent mainly on cattle for their livelihood, and to a much lesser extent on agricultural products. With its rituals and sacrifices to gods "in heaven", it had none of the idol worship. The Vedic Brahmins had gods of sun or *Mitra*, air or *Indra*, and fire or *Agni*. They had sacrifice or *yagna* using oblations into the sacred fire that they hoped would bring them wealth in cattle and grain, and success in battle. They undoubtedly ate beef and drank potent liquor and seemed to be unaware until later times of the practices of meditation and yoga. Their sacred hymns were passed down verbally in an ancient form of Sanskrit and even today are incanted word perfect by orthodox Brahmin priests to accompany temple and other rituals.

It seems, as the historians would have us believe, that the Vedic herdsmen came into contact with a native Indian culture; which had some tradition of avatar and idol worship, as well as a knowledge of an "inner spirituality. The white skinned Aryans intermingled with the dark Dravidians until only few "pure" carriers of the traditional Vedic lore remained. These few formed perhaps the backbone and ancestry of the modern Hindu Brahmins, who preach that the Vedas are Hinduism's founding true past.

Although Hindus look with great reverence on "their" Vedic history, in actual practice today's Hinduism owes perhaps more to the indigenous beliefs and religion that must have been present in India before the advent of the Aryans.

Today Brahmin pundits recite the ancient Vedic hymns at wedding ceremonies, formal functions and, of course, in temples. It is for them a livelihood, which has been inherited through their caste. Many of the Hindus who attend these rituals have no idea what the Vedic words mean as they are accustomed to worshipping Rama, Krishna or Shiva in their own vernacular.

It is much like the average churchgoer listening to a sermon or hymn in Latin. I suspected that a few of the pundits, who learnt their chants by heart, had limited ideas of the meaning of what they are actually chanting. Nevertheless to hear Vedic hymns chanted properly by a group of learned Brahmins is an invigorating and uplifting experience. There becomes apparent the marvelous connection between flowing poetry, and sonorous song that strikes a hidden chord in the listener's heart.

It was not until the end of the Vedic period that the Upanishads, with their philosophy of renunciation and introspection were written. This later scriptural wealth seems to have been influenced by a very indigenous and non-Aryan culture. The inner spiritual quest was possibly a legacy of the land in which the Aryans arrived, as it was not easily identifiable as being part of their culture as contained within the Vedic literature of sacrificial works.

The Upanishads expound a philosophy at opposite poles to that of ritualism, sacrifice, and prayers for prosperity, and state that no real happiness can be obtained by following Vedic injunctions for the promulgation of wealth and material benefits. Vedanta (or the "end" of the Vedas), is thus the system which even is "anti" the Vedic gods. However, devotion to one's guru (and in later works to one's chosen deity), is strongly advocated in Vedanta treatises as a means towards gaining self-realization. It is also accepted however that Advaita is the ultimate philosophy only for those who have purified themselves in the practices of bhakti, yoga or selfless actions.

From around the beginning of the Christian period, the Advaita concept diverged into the variations conceived by different teachers who were more devotional towards a personal God. For some sects, the individual soul was seen as separate from, and yet united with, God at one and the same time. Others felt that there was always a separate soul that never united with a Godhead. Thus evolved the various groupings of devotional Hinduism, some of which have worldwide renown today. One is the "Hare Krishna" movement which derives from a very orthodox and traditional system.

The Hindu can be an atheist, a devotee of Krishna, or a sacrificial fire worshipping follower of the Vedas, they are all Hindus. Not only that but speak to some Hindus and you will find they believe that Jesus was a Hindu saint who lived in Kashmir for a while, and that Mohammed's teachings are derived from Hindu scriptures. Hindus often see Buddhism (and other religions), as being part of *their* religion, although Buddhists, Sikhs and Jains would not subscribe easily to this view. It becomes apparent that many Hindus perceive of all religions as existing under one wide reaching umbrella. I feel that one of the reasons why Hinduism never developed a strong missionary type influence is because no cult, belief, or religion seems exceptionally different from the Hindu's own.

* Advaita - a Sanskrit word meaning non-duality or non-separation of the individual and the universal God.

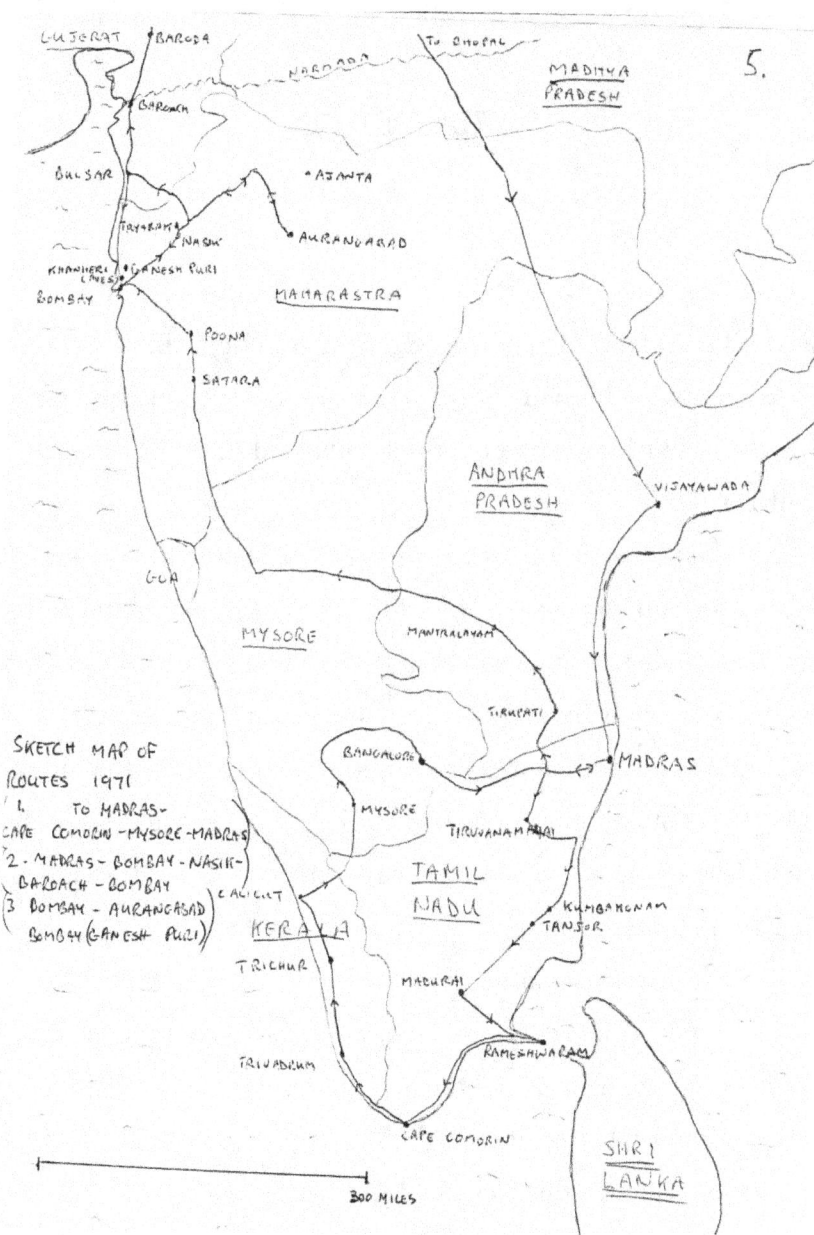

CHAPTER SIX
A Guru Lost

In my first year at the Dehra Dun ashram, I managed to assimilate a lot of new knowledge and practical skills. I could sit comfortably in meditation and had developed my knowledge about the spiritual aspects of life embodied in the Hindu culture.

Moreover, I was beginning to understand and speak Hindi, as well as practice the full lifestyle of a brahmachari. An imperceptible sequence of changes occurred within me, taking over my whole being, so that I no longer thought about myself in terms of my previous Englishman role. I rapidly became, in effect, one more addition to the millions of Indian sadhus, adopting my new personality totally and exclusively; so much so that I stopped writing to my parents and forgot about all my connections in England.

Looking back it could seem as if I allowed myself to be completely brain - washed for a very lengthy period of my life. At the time I felt that my English "self" was a handicap, which got in the way of achieving the type of experience that I wanted. Then, I needed to become a new and different person with a complete change of identity: not just a new name and different habits. As I stayed on at the ashram I took on an increasingly responsible role in the running of the place and became swamiji's "right hand man".

Swami Chaitanya Prakash Ananda preached his daily satsang at the ashram when in residence. As I improved my Hindi, I began to understand every word of these daily sermons. He also gave lectures whilst on tour in various parts of North India. These tours would last weeks or even months; and he would spend a third of the year away from Dehra Dun.

I went along with him on all the tours he did for the first two years of my stay at the ashram. Through my travels I got to know the holy pilgrimage places from the inside. We also visited towns and cities, often staying in the luxurious homes of the wealthiest devotees. In these homes swamiji was accorded a high level of respect and shown great hospitality. This was due to his high position in the hierarchy of holy men. He was not only a learned sadhu, but also a member of an orthodox sect of sannyasins, and he had elevated status even amongst other sannyasins. As well as this, his "ownership" of an established ashram made him important in terms of rank, placing him well above the many sadhus who were only resident in other's property.

One might wonder how his orthodoxy squared with having a foreign disciple traveling with him. He did, in fact, derive great pleasure from having on show one of his successfully converted "heathen foreigners". I found that I enhanced his status no end, especially as I had adopted my own role so completely. However I very gradually began to resent being a showpiece. In compensation, I found that a great deal of the respect shown to him was also showered on me. I was garlanded along with him, and his devotees also came and touched *my* feet. Best of all in my mind was the rich vegetarian food that we were served in the devotees' houses. We were invited to more lunches, dinners, teas and breakfasts than we could accommodate and often we would visit five or six homes in a row, just to give "blessings".

    The lecture tours consisted of a week or two of daily satsang in some hall before an audience of several hundred people and provided good "purses" for swamiji. Combined with the donations received on house visits, I think that a decent amount of money was collected; enough for him to embark on the construction of a second ashram in Haridwar.

    Right from the beginning of my tour experiences, I was made to give a five-minute speech in English to the assembled listeners before swamiji spoke in the lecture halls. The great majority of the audience did not understand English, but that seemed of little relevance, as I was a novelty to them. Having a fair skinned foreigner behave as their own Indian sadhus did, seemed to create considerable interest.

    In those halls, often attached to temples, the flat platforms for the speakers were raised above the audience who sat cross legged on the floor. I used to sit slightly to the rear of swamiji and to one side of the platform. I just sat on the linen covered base, whereas he always had a special square rug to sit on. I carried this wherever we went, and it was my duty to place it on the platforms before he spoke. The fact that a European chela should carry and place his rug before the assembled devotees offered him a great deal of prestige.

The schedule of the day could be very hectic whilst we were on the lecture rounds. Daily there could be two or more sessions of an hour spent sitting in the lecture halls or *bhavans*, followed by visits to up to ten homes, where swamiji would often give short talks. In the devotees' houses, the whole family would perform puja to swamiji. He became the deity and image for their ritualistic worship, and all the elements of a temple puja were used. Human form worship of the guru or of a sadhu or sannyasin is common in Hinduism.

For some of the "big names" in the world of gurus, the ceremonies on special occasions like their birthdays, can be on a large scale indeed. The throngs of disciples physically and mentally worship their guru as God, a ritual that is completely in accord with Hindu scriptural injunction.

The problem with the ideal of a guru being God incarnate is that there are many such gods due to the multiplicity of religious sects. Often rival groups of devotees will be very critical of the other group's guru, and the gurus themselves will often utter scathing remarks about their rivals. This backbiting and opposition between different sects is not an appealing aspect of Hinduism; but then conflict within Christianity and other religions is not exactly uncommon. With a wide choice of sects, it is relatively easy to change from one guru or sect to another within the Hindu fold. Some Hindus worship or revere a selection of devas, or deities, and accord their allegiance to a variety of gurus. However, more usually, a single Ishta Deva as well as a single Sat Guru holds prominence for most Hindus.

After two years at Dehra Dun, my role had gradually changed from that of student on the spiritual path to that of useful full time worker, in the temples, the gardens, and in swamiji's quarters as his personal helper. I did not really want to drift into this role, as I much preferred to sit with books, meditate, or do yoga exercises.

However, I could not continue to eat the ashram food and receive clothing and other items without some obligations to give in return. My own personal time was called upon most during lecture tours, and I found that I was increasingly expected to be some sort of personal servant. After a while, despite the benefits I received on tour, I began more and more to question my apparent exhibition role.

Instead I stopped traveling and stayed at Dehra Dun and ran the ashram while he was away.
The bonus of the tours was that I did see lots of India, (and went to many feasts). We visited Kashmir twice, Varanasi, Allahabad, Brindaban, Delhi and Amritsar, to name but a few places. We went to famous temples and pilgrimage centers, where we met all types of sadhus and stayed in a

variety of ashrams. We went to the holy fairs, (the Khumba Melas), and participated in these larger than life spectacles. We stayed in mansions and were driven to the best sightseeing spots by wealthy disciples.

I was, however, getting fed up with the elaborate proceedings that accompanied these tours, the baggage handling, (that fell to me), the ritual observances, the lack of time to myself, and the demands made on me to become the ideal chela.

So I avoided going away with swamiji after the first two years I took on most of the ashram management duties, having charge of the temples and supervision of the gardens and orchard. I would also read out the scriptures in the daily satsang sessions.

I did not sit on the elevated platform in the verandah of the ashram, but had instead my own seat and reading dais, (at floor level). I only read out the daily "lesson" and did not interpret or lecture on the scripture or subject I was speaking about. Nevertheless, I began to assume a much more important role in the eyes of the devotees who continued to visit the ashram.

Whilst not a guru when I was in charge, I savored the experience and rewards in terms of the respect and attention I received. I gave up much of the austere behavior that I had been practicing.

Before I took up my practical role in the ashram, qualifying myself for a life with more comforts, I had tried to remain as aloof as possible. Then I wanted only shelter and food only so I could allow myself, with a clear conscience, the right to give a minimal amount of my time to do ashram chores.

For one space of three months, I had engaged in a more austere and penitent lifestyle than for the other periods, although during all my first two years I lived an extremely simple life. The word used in Sanskrit for such rigorous penance is tapas, which literally means to burn or heat oneself. During a three-month period, I ate one simple meal a day only. Apart from that I drank only water: no snacks, no tea, & no milk. I did not use soap on my clothes or body, and gave up all bedding except for one sheet. I spent nearly all my time in meditation, excepting a few hours occupied in the temples and the garden. I felt like a wild savage after a while but, surprisingly in view of the hardship, I remember that period as a time of mental euphoria.

I went around with a single gray cloth around my body. It was actually a white cotton dhoti, but washing in water only had not removed the ingrained dirt. I grew my long hair into the matted locks that many sadhus sport in India. Unfortunately, my head became lice ridden and extremely unpleasant to live with, despite the use of various herbal applications. Eventually I had my head and beard shaved, and after that continued to get shaved by the barber who came in.

Sannyasins generally have shaved heads, and the vainer among them have a weekly visit from the barber to keep a shiny, "smart" image. I could generally let my hair grow for a few months before there was any risk of head lice, or prior becoming uncomfortably warm in the hot season. A shaved head as it is much more bearable in a hot climate. Usually however, except for sannyasins, a tuft of hair is left on the crown. This tuft has a religious significance, as it is the "escape" route for the soul after death.

Everyone who has a shaven head gets the job done by a barber, who in many cases has a kerb side stall, consisting mainly of an ordinary kitchen chair. Sadhus and sannyasins prefer to have a visiting barber as this is seen as more socially correct. If I can remember rightly, the cost for a full beard and head shave was less than a rupee. The cut throat type razors used never had a painful effect on the scalp and skin, even though plain soapy water was used instead of shaving cream. Incidentally, one got a toe and finger nail manicure included in the price:

Another of my austerities was in going barefoot for several years. I arrived in India without shoes and found no problems in the hot climate once the skin on my soles had hardened. However, in the first winter my soles cracked badly end the flesh inside the cracks remained very tender for months. When I went out on a cold day first thing on a frosty morning into the scrubland for ablutions, it felt as if I was walking on glass. The stiff blades of grass would dig into the cracks in the skin and pierce the tender flesh underneath. It also stung to wash my feet in cold water something I had to do umpteen times a day before entering the temples or ashram buildings.

    I was determined to persevere though and I developed cast iron soles eventually. I took to footwear again after a five years in India to avoid muck and dirt rather than painful rocks and stones. I got a pair of plastic sandals in which I could walk moderate distances. When I did some long distance walking on my later travels, I went barefoot at times as this proved more comfortable for me.

    The barefoot experience was rather marred by an occasion in Dehra Dun when I got a poisonous palm tree needle stuck in my foot. The tip of the wooden needle broke off, my foot turned septic, and I ended up in Dehra Dun hospital for a minor operation.

    The Dehra Dun hospital visit was the first of two hospital experiences for me in my first few years in India. I developed on a number of occasions a high fever of indeterminate origin. I would be laid up for a week or two feeling very ill, so ill in fact that on one trip to Varanasi I had to go into a hospital there. Mostly, however, I had a period of great disability, during which I would receive antibiotic courses from a friendly devotee doctor in Dehra Dun.

    On my first hospital visit with a septic foot, I had to have the infected part cut out under anesthetic, and then stay a week while the poisons and fever left my system. The hospital I stayed in was very poor due to its state of impoverishment. There was only one set of toilets for several floors and these were usually awash with fouling, owing to faulty, or nonexistent, plumbing. My "food" at the hospital was hot powdered milk, (donated from overseas), and I relied on meals brought in. The staff were exceptionally helpful and friendly and the treatment for me was free and often preferential.

I did feel after this experience that hospitals in India were a good place to contract diseases and I tried to keep out of them, no matter how ill I felt.

The only other hospital using western methods of medicine, in which I became a patient, was a Rama Krishna Mission place in Varanasi. I developed a dreadful fever whilst staying with in an ashram near the banks of the Ganges. Varanasi is for many the major center of spiritual life in North India. It is full of temples, pilgrims and sadhus, and is the place to go for Hindus who believe that they are near death. Dying in Varanasi means instant heaven for the pious soul who has moved there to spend his or her last days by the sacred Ganges. Varanasi is full of *ghats*: bathing steps leading down into the river. There the multitude have their dip and say their prayers standing in the holy waters sins.

I had been bathing in the ghats and drinking the sacred waters along with thousands of pilgrims and suspect that here was the source of my illness. Gallons of raw sewage are pumped into the Ganges at Vasanasi, as well as the effluent from hundreds of dhobi washermen, who bring their bundles to wash on stone slabs near the river. Purifying the waters may be, be, but clean, never: There is a blind pride that shuts off the realities of squalid surroundings from the mysticism and beauty of religious beliefs. I know I had the same attitude at that time.

The hospital in Varanasi was quite pleasant and clean. I was looked after well, and, after ten unbearable days of fever and pain, 'I was able to get up and walk about on shaky legs. The only other "hospital" visit after that was to a, nature cure center, where treatment consisted mainly of fasts, enemas, mud packs and hip baths. Along with a succession of fevers I had suffered a number of stomach complaints.

When I went down with one of them in a town near Bareilly. I had a temperature of 104°F. (40°C.), accompanied by vomiting and constipation. Nearby was a natural cure center and they were keen to treat me for free as long as I wished. I guess they wished to prove the efficacy of their treatments, and having an English sadhu patient was a good advertisement for them.

I was given a room and had a full time helper or assistant who was paid for by one of the wealthy devotees. I was put on a diet of vegetable juice only and during the day was given a variety of mud pack and hip bath treatments. My helper proved to be an absolute necessity as my treatment continued for well over a month, by which time I was too weak to stand up and could not use my eyes for reading. My elevated temperature remained for a month, until one day I was able to have a bowel motion, and passed what seemed like blobs of iron. It might have been some chronic blockage in my stomach, which caused fever by allowing an accumulation of toxins.

At this stage I had been lying in a semi coma for a week, and can remember that I lived in a pleasant dream like state continually. It is peculiar to relate but in my dream state I was living in South West London as an antique dealer who dealt in old Guns and Armour. In my dream, I travelled around buying and selling, and had a shop at Hampton Court. It was a very vivid and weird experience, which went on continually far over a week. I could not remember being washed and fed during this period such was the extent of my feebleness.

Two weeks after the sudden easing of my fever and the resumption of bowel functions, the staff at the nature cure center still wanted to keep me there for a while longer on my liquid diet. They wished to make sure my cure was complete: I was already a bag of bones and the devotees in Bareilly thought I would die if I stayed on. Eventually I was removed to the home of the devotee who had paid for my nurse. I began to recover there on a diet that graduated slowly from milk to solid food.

I found that I had a huge appetite and could digest anything and everything that I could get my hands on. I rapidly recovered my strength and for years to follow had top health, considering the dangers of my Indian environment. I feel that the natural method of treatment used was worthwhile for its results and it gave me a lot of faith in the use of such methods as opposed to medicinal drugs.

    The natural fasting treatment may have been lengthy and debilitating, but the reward was a dramatic improvement in my susceptibility to disease. I was able happily to drink any non-boiled water and eat food from any source, without illness, for the next five years.

I gave up most of my austere practices after my second year at Dehra Dun, and went almost in the opposite direction. I say almost, because there was a limit to the availability of comforts and luxuries in the ashram.

    When I began to take an active role in the running of the place', I started to use whatever facilities were available. I wore good quality dhotis, ate two proper meals a day and had tea and milk with snacks - a luxurious lifestyle: When I had the run of the place to myself, I had an even freer hand with my eating and sleeping habits. I began to have meals cooked for me by devotees, and had access to make myself a snack or drink whenever I felt like it. Gradually I created comfortable quarters for myself in one of the side buildings and eventually even had the use of an indoor toilet!

    Food and its preparation began to interest me more than my other jobs around the place. I learnt to cook basic North Indian food over gas, coal or wood fires. Wood fires always meant that a lot of time and energy were spent on the utensils. The large brass pots had to be smeared underneath with clay and water to prevent burning, and the top halves had to be cleaned with water and ashes to remove the soot after use. For a fireplace, few bricks sufficed, although more elaborate ones were built for permanent use.

To cook the rotis and chappaties, a concave iron griddle is placed on top of the wood fire. When the circular flat bread is cooked it is then held in tongs and turned sideways in some embers, so that the edges cook properly and the bread fluffs up. This bread is usually eaten hot straight from the griddle. A fairly orthodox vegetarian family would sit down around the cook, usually a female of the household. One could get a wooden board to sit on, cross legged, and the circular metal eating plates were placed in front on the ground. The rotis are passed directly from the fire to the plate and the other dishes of dhal and vegetables are replenished by the cook as needed. Usually the women of a, Hindu house will serve the men and children first, and only after they have finished and left will the women sit down to eat.

Many men did cook for themselves in India because of the Hindu caste system which rules out inter caste cooking. For instance, young men at college may each prepare their own meals separately, on a small coal or paraffin stove. Thus men away from home, or in college, or without their wives, have to learn to cook for themselves.

In ashrams or large houses there is sometimes a male cook, usually of the Brahmin caste. Any other caste under their rules, can eat food prepared by him. Each caste can eat food prepared by its own or by a higher one only. In the Dehra Dun ashram we sometimes had a sadhu or Brahmin pundit staying who would cook for the main kitchen, with swamiji's being separate, and anyone could eat his preparations. Sometimes for a few days I would be the cook and strangely enough, nobody demurred from eating my food, although people of high caste whom I fed would have normally refused a non-Brahmin's cooking. The fact that I was fair skinned put me almost automatically in the "high caste" league, especially when I spoke and behaved like a Hindu.

In our ashram, one or more of the female devotees would stay on after satsang to help prepare food and do some cleaning. Most of their time was spent in swamiji's kitchen and living quarters, but they would cook for any other ashram visitors and residents if necessary and if acceptable by caste rules. They did all this without pay or reward for their belief was that the service of holy men would give them rewards in heaven and the afterlife.

I did settle into a very routine, and ritualistic, existence. It was an entirely alien lifestyle compared with my English upbringing. I did not feel that I was English, as I spoke and even dreamt in Hindi. My daily routine was orthodox Hindu, and I performed my daily ablutions, prayers and temple worship, using the correct Sanskrit hymns according to the scriptural rules.

Although I was becoming more enmeshed in ritual Hinduism, I was drifting further from my original interests: yoga, meditation, and Vedanta. I spent my free time delving into obscure books concerning the worship of the less popular deities, and the philosophies of minor sects of Hinduism.

At this time, I also became more and more interested in Shakti worship. Shakti is the female aspect of divine power and consciousness. The goddess whose image is most well-known and popular in India is Durga, a many armed figure seated on a tiger. Kali is less widely worshipped, except in Bengal. She has a dark - skinned image and is depicted as holding a sword, carrying a severed head and wearing a necklace of skulls. She is seen as a wild, savage goddess of destruction and in Calcutta, her most famous temple is to be found.

Other forms of Shakti include Saraswati (the goddess of learning or knowledge) and Lakshmi, (the goddess of wealth). The power of Shakti is also recognized as the body dwelling *Kundalini*, the "coiled serpent" power that dwells at the base of the spine, waiting to be awakened by the right mantra or guru. When Kundalini rises in the body, the energy is perceived to travel upwards through various chakra centers, until it arrives at the thousand petal lotus flower in the crown of the head.

With full awakening, the yogi is supposed to drink the nectar of divine bliss from this chakra, and be elevated to a superconscious state of total knowledge. I was not to understand the mysteries of Kundalini until my later years in India, although I did try out various mantras used in Shakti worship.

I had been initiated by swamiji into various mantras associated with Vishnu and Shiva, but nothing had been taught to me about Shakti. I realized that swamiji himself performed a lot of Durga puja and this was his favorite deity. However he would not initiate me into any mantras in this line and told me that the ones I had were sufficient. It was after this that I began to use my own initiative as far as choice of sadhana and deities were concerned.

I started to study the relevant scriptural treatises (in Hindi and Sanskrit) and chose my own mantras, discarding the ones given to me by swamiji. I did not tell him of my new interests because at this time, three and a half years after my arrival, I was tending to go my own way in many other respects. Without making things too obvious, I avoided as much contact with him as possible. I had almost been convinced by him at one time that I should seek Indian citizenship.

Now I was thinking about leaving India, altogether I still wished to complete my studies and investigation into Shakti and other paths to self-realization, and I also wanted to do a little travel in India on my own.

As I started to drop hints about my wish to leave and return to England, I found that swamiji and his devotees became quite fervent in their efforts to change my mind. Many arguments were put forward to try and persuade me to continue in my role at the ashram. The strongest incentive was dangled in front of me by swamiji, who began to tell people that I would be his successor, and thus the head or guru of the ashram. I was told that I could become a very powerful figure with control over an ever increasing amount of property.

    I was, however, as unwilling to become a sannyasin, as I was becoming more interested in getting married and settling for a conventional lifestyle. I did want to first travel the rest of India, particularly the South, and meet other gurus, sadhus and holy men. It was made obvious to me that if I did leave for other pastures, I would be guilty of unfathomable treachery both to swamiji and the ashram's devotees. They had, in their words, done so much for me over the years.

    I did feel bad for a while, because of harboring ideas about "deserting" swamiji, but I became increasingly resentful about the pressures put on me to try and make me stay. I began to plan my departure in more detail and retrieved my passport from swamiji's safe, saying that I had to send it to the High Commission for some changes. In fact I only wanted to keep it because I felt that some people were going to try very hard to keep me in Dehra Dun. After all, I knew that it would be a great loss of face for swamiji and the ashram if I were to depart to seek a new guru. Owing to my resentment of the psychological pressures put on me, I began to skip or alter some of my daily routine. When nobody was around I would "short cut" on temple duties, and my sleeping and eating habits started to incline towards indolence. I not only mentally disliked the feelings of being controlled and manipulated by swamiji, but began outwardly to rebel against my role as his chela.

Looking back over my years in the Dehra Dun ashram, I feel that in many ways I had arrived there as an extremely susceptible person. To a degree, I allowed myself to be brain washed. On arrival I had been traveling in an impoverished manner for nearly a year. I was young, at eighteen, and had smoked a lot of cannabis, which had dulled my mind to extent than I had not realized.

Later in India I met other Europeans who became involved with a variety of sects, cults, and guru, often when the drugs proved unfulfilling. Conditions of homelessness, poverty or social alienation can compound feelings of isolation from the "normal" world. If something appears which offers the individual a sense of belonging, then the conversion can be dramatic. Americans who had become disciples of various gurus, and lived the ashram life, had been heavily into drug scene using L.S.D. in particular. (Especially in San Francisco).

Does heavy drug use leave one unnaturally open to a variety of spiritual "conversions" or enrolment into religious organizations? Is it because of a deep sense of isolation from a society? Are dramatic conversions harmful or dangerous to the individual or society? My own period of rigid religious belief benefited me in many ways and ultimately I emerged as the master of my own beliefs with a better ability to deal with life in general. Possible without that grounding and discipline I would have ended up institutionalized or dead! The conversion to extreme religious attitudes may be no more "dangerous" than the holding of strong political views. I could not therefore advocate de-programming, although I can sympathize with some of the motives of those who seek this.

CHAPTER SEVEN
A Sadhu's Life

When I came to leave Dehra Dun for good nearly four and a half years had passed since my arrival. I left surreptitiously at night, running away from this home as I had done before in England when aged seventeen.

I was not able to communicate my wish to leave and go my own way to swamiji and his devotees. I knew I would be heavily criticized, even prevented from leaving somehow, and could leave only with huge difficulty.

I was not mentally strong enough to stand up for my own wishes and walk out with head held high, even if I was abused for doing so. I would be accused of deserting the place and people that had nurtured me for over four years. Although I had just walked into the role of being swamiji's disciple, I did not have the heart to just walk openly back out again. In fact I wanted to say that I wished to have no more to do with him, or the ashram, and possibly Hinduism.

I intended at that stage to return to England and resume life there where I had left off. However, once I had departed from Dehra Dun and begun to feel "free" again, I found that a sadhu's lifestyle still had a lot to offer. I decided to see a bit more of India and the incredible variety of people and places that were awaiting me. I wished also to seek out some other gurus and holy men, as I was dissatisfied with what I had achieved spiritually so far.

I left Dehra Dun with the help of a young Indian who had come to stay at the ashram for a few weeks. He was traveling around India seeking out various swamis and gurus in order to gain an insight into the world of holy men, with a view to becoming a sadhu himself. He came from Bombay where he had held a clerical type job and had made the acquaintances of a number of hippy type Europeans.

He was unusually well versed in modern Western trends and held very independent ideas about Hinduism. Having won some money on the horses, (or so he said), he had left his job and flat and taken to traveling the country. We had long conversations together during which I confided my ideas and feelings. He told me that, in his opinion, I was wasting my time staying in the ashram and recommended that I left Dehra Dun for good on the night train to Delhi. He offered to come to the station with me and cover my tracks if possible after my departure. As swamiji was away on a lecture tour at that time I decided to wait until a few days before his return, so that I would not inconvenience the running of the ashram. On the chosen day I made up a package of stuffed breads to sustain me for a few days. I carried a few hundred rupees that I had saved from various personal gifts.

Thus I set off once more into the unknown, by catching the night train to Delhi, which arrived in the early hours. I then immediately purchased a ticket to Vijayawada near Madras, for fifty rupees, third class. A thousand mile, three day train journey for the equivalent of then three pounds sterling! I felt the chill of that winter's day as the train moved south, to take me in the next few days across a large portion of India, into the non-Hindi speaking state of Andra Pradesh. I had chosen Vijayawada for no particular reason other than it seemed a good place to throw off the scent. I figured that some of swamiji's devotees might follow to try and persuade me to return.

Swamiji was due back in Dehra Dun about the time that I reached Andra Pradesh and I thought that he might try something to thwart me in my travels.
Nearing Vijayawada I got talking in English to a local Hindu who told me that one of the Shankaracharyas was staying in some temple grounds in the town, and that he was a holy person well worth visiting. The original Shankaracharya of the ninth century A.D. was a learned sannyasin who expounded and enlarged upon the philosophy of Vedanta in his scholarly works. Several centers of learning were formed by him, each with a headman titled Shankaracharya, who passed on his post to one of his foremost sannyasin disciples who was an orthodox Brahmin. The tradition has continued, and for some Hindus the head of each center is similar in status to the position of say an archbishop or Cardinal in the Christian church.

The Shankaracharyas are most powerful in South India, where orthodox Brahmins have control over the temples.

Sannyasins ordained by Shankaracharyas have a much more rigid set of rules and observances than the majority who follow less orthodox sects. These *danda*, (staff carrying), swamis are not meant to handle money, stay in houses, or eat food not obtained in the prescribed manner. Their lifestyle is rather similar to that of some Buddhist monks. However, the majority of sannyasins in India tend to stay in both ashrams and houses. Many accumulate money and luxuries.

I went to the temple where the Shankaracharya was staying, and was welcomed by some of his Brahmin devotees, given a meal, and shown to a queue for audience with His Holiness; a young, robust South Indian. He was sitting cross legged on a rather plush throne raised off the ground. Next to it stood the file of devotees waiting in line for a brief darshan. As I came up in turn before him, he asked me what I was doing in Vijayawada. I told him that I had run away from Dehra Dun since I no longer got on with my guru there. He seemed quite sympathetic, suggested that I spend the night in the temple buildings and gave me the address and telephone number of a Brahmin family in Madras. He explained that this family had looked after an English sadhu before and would be keen to meet me.

Whilst I was in the temple grounds, a young man approached me and said that he was a disciple of Swami Chaitanya Prakasha Ananda. He told me that he had received a telegram from Dehra Dun, although he did not say exactly what it stated. I must have been traced through the ticket office in Delhi, amazing considering the thousands of travelers thronging through that station daily. How then was I tracked down so quickly to this particular temple in a very large town? The young man seemed a bit vague and unsure of himself as he realized that I was now the guest of the Shankaracharya, the highest officially acknowledged holy man in the area. He asked me where I was going next and whether I would like to visit his house. When I gave rather evasive replies he seemed to become nervous and then left abruptly, and that was the last I heard from Dehra Dan. Their contacts in South India were limited!

    I caught the train to Madras, another two hundred miles south, and rang the telephone number given to me in Vijayawada. Bala Subramaniya spoke to me and told me to catch the bus to his house. I was given a warm welcome by him and his family. They had got to know well the English sadhu mentioned earlier who wore only one cloth, kept absolutely no possessions and did not handle money. He spoke perfect Tamil and traveled all over Tamil Nadu (Madras State), visiting his numerous devotees and friends. His lifestyle was unorthodox by sadhu standards as he would hob nob with High Court Judges and film stars, eating non vegetarian food when offered and even accepting the odd cigar or peg of whisky. He was, however, held in very high regard by some very orthodox Brahmins, who felt that he was on a very elevated spiritual plane. When I met him briefly in Madras, my impression was of a sincere and very dynamic person.

The Brahmin family of Balu, (to use his nickname), followed strict caste rules. Thus, even though I was made very welcome, I was given food on plantain leaves, so that I would not "pollute" their metal eating plates. They were very pleased to see my easy acceptance of their caste observances and gave me lots of advice about temples and yogis to visit in South India. Balu prepared a lengthy itinerary for me on paper and gave me also one hundred rupees to help me on my way.

He hoped that his association with my holy pilgrimage would bring him something in return. He wanted his rewards in this life if possible as he wished to gain promotion within his insurance company: I was very enthusiastic about the trip, as I knew I could purchase bus and train tickets at least as far as the southernmost tip of India. Food and accommodation needs did not worry me. I was confident I could survive even without money, as I would now live as a fully-fledged itinerant holy man. Nevertheless, I did not want too much hassle with hitch hiking or ticket less travel. I was unwilling to undergo too much hardship just for the sake of being a wandering sadhu, and I kept the idea of returning to England at some stage if life became too difficult.

Whilst in Madras I got my first real taste of the South Indian lifestyle, which is different in many respects from that of North India. For a start, a lot of men in the city wore the dhoti, which was not so commonly seen in urban areas in the north, where Western style trouser and cotton pajama like wear were more popular. Even in the small towns and villages of North India the traditional white cloth apparel was then only favored by older folk and land workers.

In Madras, however, even men working in smart offices would wear long, wrap - around white dhotis. Often these would be turned up at the bottom and hitched above the knees, easy to manage in rain for instance, or when running for a bus. The general retention of caste rules and traditional practices was more pronounced or severe in the South. For example, banana leaves were frequently used as plates as they are much "purer" than the North Indian style metal *thalis*. In Balu's house, everyone ate sitting on the floor and did not drink water directly from their metal cups. Even with the metal tea "glasses" the lips were not meant to touch the sides. Instead one had to invert the cup a few inches above the mouth and let the fluid trickle in that way. For tea and coffee a rimmed, saucer like dish was used in which the liquid was cooled first, before being poured into the mouth.

According to Balu, Brahmins in the South were very strict, never eating outside caste rules, and observing scriptural injunctions rigorously. Later I was to find it difficult to get into some South Indian temples even when I said that I was a Hindu. In one, they took me to a manager's office, where I was told that as a foreigner I would have to have a signed warrant from a magistrate proving I was a Hindu! They were certainly suspicious in the Southern temples then about any fair skinned person, even if dressed in the garb of a holy - man. In North India, I was never refused entry to any temple, let alone regarded with suspicion. More often than not, I was welcomed with open arms like V.I.P. Things were to prove very different at some of my stops in the South.

Another difference that became immediately apparent to me was the food. Roti and chappaties were almost unheard of; rice being the staple diet of the southern half of India. A meal began with a portion of rice placed on a banana leaf on top of which was ladled a thick lentil and vegetable soup. This had to be mulched together and scooped up with the fingers. Once finished, another portion of rice was served, accompanied by *rasam*, a thin, peppery soup. One had to be quite dexterous then, otherwise the rasam would flow over the leaf and trickle onto the floor. Watery curds accompanied a final serving of rice, and that was the basic meal apart from little side dishes of pickles or sweetmeats.

At all my meals in South India, I noticed a greater concern about pollution by touch. The person serving the food was very careful not to let the ladle touch your leaf, or to let their clothes touch your body. After a meal I often had to fold up the used leaf plate and deposit it in a bin, even if I was the house guest. Amongst most families in North India, it would be unthinkable to let a guest move an empty plate. They would often bring a bowl, water and towel so that you could rinse your mouth and hands on the spot, whilst your plate was whisked away.

In a South Indian Brahmin's house, this sort of thing would be considered a very bad, impure practice. I did form a definite bias towards certain Northern States. This was because I received far less hospitality and a more aloof response from people whilst traveling the Southern States. There I even found some hostility shown towards me, although, to be fair, 1 met many extremely friendly, generous and helpful people. Later, back in the North, especially in Gujerat, I was to encounter open arms type hospitality everywhere. More and more frequently, I was made to feel one of the family, and invited to stay in many homes.

The languages of South India are completely different from the northern ones. Hindi, Bengali, Gujerati and others have roots in Aryan India and hence have a connection with European languages. The Dravidian languages are a world apart, and Tamil, Telegu in Andra Pradesh, Malayalam in Kerala, and Kannada in Mysore, have no similarities with Hindi and its associated dialects. It is like the difference between English and Swahili.

According to some historians, the Dravidian culture is an older culture than the Aryan one and was indigenous throughout India before being pushed south by the invading Aryan tribes. Southerners can dislike Hindi, especially as it has been pushed on them on them as the national language at times. English is therefore spoken widely in particularly in business matters. Kerala has the highest level of literacy in India and speakers of perfect English, having the largest number of graduates. Poverty and large unemployment figures did not guarantee a job however.

From Madras I headed south on the first leg of my mapped out tour of South India's great temples and ashrams. I had transport costs and after that it would have to be up to providence. My first stop would be at Tiruvanamalai to visit a well-known ashram where Ramana Maharshi had spent the last thirty years of his life (until 1950). He was a yogi of few words who reclined motionless for hours on a simple couch, at the foot of which devotees sat and bathed in the tranquility that he emanated. He told his followers to find the Inner Self within and to ask "Who am I?"

I had read books about him and his teachings and was impressed by stories about him. He drew, like a magnet, spiritual seekers from many different countries and his ashram was flourishing when I visited nearly twenty-five years after his death. It continues to this day, attracting people from all over the world to his tranquil shrine. European royalty were amongst those who visited the ashram to soak up the ever-present atmosphere of peace that seems as strong then as it was during the Maharshi's life.

I stayed three days and spent most of my time meditating in the room where the Master's couch is preserved; where visitors sit as they did in the days when he was alive. In that simple, wooden floored room there was an atmosphere of indescribable calmness. It was like a heavy haze of tranquility permeated every corner. There were always people entering and leaving the room, touching the couch, standing in silence, or sitting for a while. Yet to me the peace seemed undisturbed by any comings and goings. That was also how it was described as being when Ramana Maharshi was alive to sit or recline on his couch in that room.

The ashram was run by a friendly and efficient band of helpers, who looked after the needs of the numerous visitors. There were communal meal arrangements and simple accommodation for all, paid for as in all such places by the donations of devotees. I am sure that Ramana Maharshi's ashram will exist with its natural uncontrived harmony for eternity.

I moved on from Tiruvannamalai with the intention of making a stop at a small ashram twenty miles away. I was delayed in leaving due to visiting temples in the town, and eventually found myself a few miles short of my destination by nightfall. I started to walk in the dark along a traffic free road, passing a small village. On the outskirts two drunks stopped me. One pulled out a knife and started waving it at me. I think the drunks were surprised at meeting a white skinned person in the dark, and also one who could not speak their language. They might have been as scared as I was, but nothing further happened and they went on their way, towards the village.

I resolved not to wander around at night in strange and isolated areas. I had already broken away from family in England and now from Dehra Dun. If I had died in a remote area, or had been thrown into a river, I would have disappeared without trace. There are many foreigners today in India who have changed their name and lifestyle and have vanished as far as their home connections are concerned. These people live, and sometimes die, unknown to their previous friends and relatives. They may number thousands and belong to many different countries, but they are all living as sadhus or even ageing hippies.

I reached the small ashram that I had on my "list", but the resident swami and guru was away. I was made welcome by some helpers there and after spending the night, set off southwards to begin visiting the huge major temples in Khumbakonam, Tanjore and Madura. I managed to visit and be allowed into the inner temples of all the major shrines, although my status as a bona fide Hindu was queried by quite a few of the temple Brahmins.

The immense South Indian temples are typified by Meenakshi in Madura. It is a fortress like place, with several sets of high walls, each surrounding a courtyard. In the courtyards of such temples there are tanks and pools where one has a ritual bath. The deities in these huge places are metal, marble or stone figures completely covered with gold, silver, silks and jewels. Sometimes several hundred Brahmins live, earn their livelihood or are supported by such temple properties.

Such temples are very rich and powerful, and the deities installed within are treated as if they were human kings and queens. They are fed, bathed, and put to bed, all in a ritualistic sense, to the accompaniment of hymn chanting, bells, drums and pipes. Members of the public come to these various pujas at appropriate times of the day, and make their obeisances and offerings. In the evening there will often be a perambulation puja, when a small figurine of the deity is taken around in a palanquin carried by Brahmin priests, to the accompaniment of much music, chanting and incense burning.

I found the atmosphere in these temples to be mesmerizing and fascinating, especially at the puja times. The color, the noise, and the throng of people stirred up deep subconscious (and perhaps primitive) feelings within me. Although it was pure ritual and idol worship, divorced from the realities of the ordinary world, I felt that it offered a fantasy like experience which is at least better than, say, drugs or alcohol. Apart from the interesting experience I obtained of temple life, I found that my visits often proved beneficial in a practical way. At some temples I was given the temple *prasad** in the form of a rice ball and lentil meal from the temple kitchens. As they often cooked for a hundred or so priests, it was easy for them to distribute leaf wrapped meals to visitors and sadhus. Usually the visiting pilgrims purchased the prasad packages but I was often given one free.

*Prasad - a Sanskrit word literally meaning "gift of the gods". Ritually offered food.

I was approached on a number of occasions by local Brahmins as soon as I stepped into a temple's grounds and offered a meal at their houses. It was part of these Brahmins' sadhana to find and feed a sadhu or holy man each day. By this they hoped to earn punya or merit to be enjoyed in the afterlife. Thus most days I was to get enough food to allay my hunger and keep me going. For the nights it was easy enough to just lie down in a corner of a temple's grounds. It was warm, even hot at night, and the only problem was that of mosquitoes.

I reached Rameshwasam by train with the last of my rupees spent on the ticket, and wondered how I would now fare, being as I was, at the southernmost tip of India. I wanted to continue my planned circuit to Cape Comorin, Kerala, Mysore and then back to Madras. I knew it might be difficult as I never begged or asked for food. In theory a sadhu or sannyasin could go begging and knocking on doors asking for alms. I abhorred this idea and could not bring myself to ask for food no matter how hungry I felt. I was prepared to eat only what was given freely, as I knew it was the way that the most respected sadhus and mahatmas had lived.

On the spur of the moment I joined the queue on the beach, which led to a man seated at a desk in an open sided shelter. I wanted to see if I could get into Shri Lanka, and this was "Immigration". The man wanted to know how much money I had, and on hearing that I had none, asked me what I proposed to do in Shri Lanka. I gave the name and address of a swami with an ashram there, which seemed to be familiar to the official. However, he pointed to a couple of fair skinned backpackers in the queue and said, "They all have to have twenty dollars before they can enter, so I don't see how I can make an exception for you". It was probably a good thing that I could not get into Shri Lanka because it was a big detour to make!

I continued my journey, going westwards towards Cape Comorin to visit the large temple of Kanyakumari, the goddess in the form of a young virgin. I had a truck lift for about half the journey and then started to walk along the road, which passed near seaside fishing villages. I noticed that in this area Christians inhabited many of the villages. There were no temples, but plenty of churches and signs pointing to Christian schools and other enterprises. Here along the coast and all the way through Kerala State there were lots of Christians.

They were mostly Roman Catholics, who had been established for many centuries since the arrival of missionaries and saints in these parts. Christianity took roots easily here. The Brahmin controlled Hindu hierarchy was a distant world for large numbers of the so-called low caste, black skinned local population. They quickly found more affinity in the brotherhood of the Christian faith. The simple fisher folk were not interested in being virtually outcastes within the racist Brahmin dominated Hindu system.

In the past, lower Hindu castes in South India were considered so wretched by the higher castes that they had to step aside whenever a Brahmin came near. A Brahmin touched by even the shadow of an outcaste would have to take a ritual bath. If a Brahmin eating a meal merely saw somebody considered unclean, then the meal would be thrown away. There existed a social structure rather similar to a slave and master system. The higher castes could commit murder and get away with it under caste laws of those times.

I noticed that, unlike in the North, there seemed to be quite a color distinction between the Brahmins of the South and the rest of the populace. Many Brahmins here had quite fair skin. According to some ancient history books, it would seem that the Brahmins of the South are descended from the fair skinned Northern Aryans. In North India, there was an almost homogenous mixing of the Aryan invaders and the local population. In the South it could seem that the Aryan Brahmin invaders remained much more aloof from the very dark skinned local Dravidian population. With the Brahmin domination came an apartheid system.

Kerala became much less of a Hindu stronghold compared to other states. They had communist governments in power there, and land was taken from the once powerful Brahmin landowners. The Brahmin castes in this part of the world can be quite snooty and ultra-orthodox. In those years, considerable anti Brahmin feeling had been expressed by the outcastes and by the Christians. I found that even sadhus are not welcomed by some of the ultra-conservative priestly castes here, unless they are Brahmins and have been ordained into the orthodox sannyasin sects. To me, Brahmins in this part of

India who looked down upon the masses got what they deserved. I heard whilst I was in the South that there had even been processions held by anti-Hindu groups, where figures of Hindu deities had been paraded in carts and hit with sandals, whilst people sang crude songs. In one town I visited, there was a Christian led march protesting about alleged Brahmin injustices. A large police force had assembled in case of trouble.

    I walked ten miles or so, passing lots of small Christian villages without seeing a single temple. Then a man approached me and introduced himself as a local teacher and a Hindu, the only one for miles around. He invited me back to his house and I rested my tired legs while his wife prepared a large vegetarian meal for me, my first food of that day.

    Whilst I was in his house that evening, several local fishermen came to see me, being curious to meet a white skinned, foreign sadhu. Most of them smelt strongly of *arack*, a gin distilled from the toddy juice of palm trees. They were friendly enough and invited me to go for a fish curry at one of their homes the next day. I declined their offer as gracefully as I could, being unwilling to eat non vegetarian food. I stayed the night with the Hindu family and left feeling well refreshed from my previous day's tiredness.

    I reached Cape Comorin by bus, courtesy of the Hindu teacher, and had darshan of the goddess at the temple. This was a somewhat hidden goal for me, as I had this devotion since Dehra Dun of seeing God as the Goddess. I probably was somewhat shy of the inner feeling or attraction I had towards the Kanya Kumari incarnation of the Goddess. I think I preferred this goddess above all but because of my human attraction to that female form as a young virgin,

I felt embarrassed and confused that this could also be my divine deity. I made my obeisance to the small idol in the temple after joining the throng, but rather than staying and feeling "at home", I felt impelled to get away fast and move a long way away! I was puzzled about this but could not understand what was going on for me in a psychological sense. (It did take another thirty years to understand the dynamics of my human and spiritual conflicts)

The place had a nice, scenic, seaside location, but I was restless to move on, and walked out of town towards the north. The road lay through the, by now, familiar coastal scenery. Coconut and banana trees stretched for miles, interspersed with groves of the toddy palm. The latter produces a white, fleshy fruit and is also tapped for liquor, which is refreshing and nutritious when first collected, but which rapidly ferments to form a mildly alcoholic drink.

Seeing all these fruit trees I was tempted to climb over the fences and see what I could get, but there always seemed to be somebody nearby. When I stopped once and peered over a fence in a seemingly deserted spot, I was shouted at by a voice from within the trees. There is a large population in Kerala, even by Indian standards. They are packed into a densely occupied strip along the coast, where a majority are poor. The fruit business does require a lot of labor, but there is no great profit in it for the average smallholder or farmer, who may have only a scrap of land.

After some difficulty with getting truck lifts, I reached Trivandrum, where I stayed a few days in the ashram of a sadhu who had a local following. After moving north and finding travel still rather difficult, I discovered a Ramakrishna Mission near Trichur where I spent a most pleasant week.

It was basically a boarding school for poor children, staffed and run by swamis of the Mission. The Ramakrishna Mission, well known in India for its philanthropic activities, had set up some schools in Kerala, where they were developing a good reputation for their combined spiritual endeavors and voluntary works. Some of the very public who were against the orthodox Brahmin stance, held the Mission and its swamis in high regard.

I visited the ashram of a well-known female yogini who lived near the Mission. She was not regarded by the educated and erudite swamis as being a self-realized soul, but I found her charisma and personality intriguing and radiant. The ashram in which she lived consisted of a number of thatch and reed huts, kept very clean, and looking homely and attractive. The yogini was a well-proportioned, youngish woman with cropped hair, dressed in flowing saffron robes. I was immediately impressed by a welcoming smile from a face that positively beamed with joy.

Through one of her devotees acting as interpreter I was told her story. She was born into a low caste local family who were small landholders. As a teenager she fell ill and the doctor diagnosed cancer, telling her that it was unlikely that she would live long. At that time she started fasting and practicing meditation. Her meditation sessions became lengthy trance like states and she stopped eating altogether. According to her devotees, she had lived for five years on a water only diet. Her body swelled up to large proportions and the "cancer" disappeared. I did not particularly credit the story about her diet or lack of it, but was impressed by her bubbling vitality and by the strong sense of peace that she emanated. I had no doubts whatever that the spiritual level she was at was a very happy one. Her presence gave me a strong sense of wellbeing. I felt slightly overcome and even dizzy for the duration of my visit.

So far, to that day, I had met a variety of swamis and holy men. Some of them were very learned and pious, but all had only an intellectual grasp of the state of self-realization. They had all seemed to me to be lacking in any strong outward or external signs of being perfected souls. When I talked to the head swami back at the mission about the yogini, he was somewhat dismissive. I got the feeling that he was a bit jealous as he went on about how much he had studied, and how important the correct understanding of self-knowledge was.

I encountered similar attitudes later, when sannyasins of some stature and erudition spoke about popular gurus or yogis, especially if the latter were low caste. They used to refer to such mahatmas with respectful phrases, but a condescending attitude could often be discerned. I wished that I had asked to stay in the yogini's ashram for a while, but at the time I was restless to see more places and meet a wide variety of India's holy men (and now women). It was certainly my first encounter with a female who had an ashram, although I knew that there were some very powerful female gurus in India. The numbers of sadhunis and swaminis* were however small compared with the numbers of holy - men.

*Sadhunis and swaminis - female sadhus and swamis.

    I moved on through Kerala into Mysore. Sometimes I slept in temple grounds where, if I were lucky, I would get a meal from the temple kitchens or from the pujari. I was invited to stay in a number of houses, both humble and well appointed. I managed to get some rides on trucks and was occasionally given money for a bus ticket. When I left the Ramakrishna Mission for instance, the head swami gave me the addresses of some other ashrams and that of another Mission where I also stayed a few days. In addition, he gave me some money, which bought me several days' bus tickets.

    I never asked for money or food. I never had to because of the fact that it is so normal for an Indian to ask all sorts of personal questions of a stranger passing by. Quite often somebody would just come up and ask me who I was, and where I was going. Then as my story unfolded, I was asked how

I managed for food and money. Half the time, the conversation would turn into an invitation to visit somebody's house or I would be directed towards a hospitable local temple.

If I stayed in somebody's house, I would be obliged to tell the tale of my travels and background to an audience of family and neighbors, with perhaps one person translating my English or Hindi. To some I was good entertainment value, as many people I met had little connection with the world outside their village and caste. When I went back into northern Hindi speaking areas I found that if I stayed in a small village, half the population would come and invite me into their houses. Everyone wanted to know how the fair skinned Englishman had come to be a wandering sadhu.

From Mysore city I headed north into an area where there are relatively large numbers of Jains. Here were some of their pilgrimage places, including the fifty one foot high stone statue of a Jain saint at Sravana Belgola.

I found it difficult to get any lifts here and one day walked twenty miles in the sun. I had lost my sandals in Kerala and ended the day with very sore feet, along with total exhaustion. I was lucky in finding a temple with a friendly sadhu in residence, and that night had my first food of the day. I found the mat provided to be a very comfortable base on which to sleep away my tiredness. Indeed I was becoming well used to sleeping on bare concrete or earth if necessary.

In another village I was the guest of a Jain family for a few days, and leant a little of their culture. Jainism is an indigenous sect, which originated at the time of Dravidian India and came to the fore with the advent of Mahavira, a contemporary of Buddha. Many Hindus believe that Jainism (like Buddhism) is an offshoot of their own religion, although Jains did not seem to accept this view and kept a strong identity. They are strict about the rule of nonviolence (ahimsa) and avoid occupations like farming, because they believe that even the uprooting of plant life is a sort of violence. There are some who wear a mask over their mouth to avoid harming any microorganisms. They do however engage in commerce and money lending and are very good at it.

The Jains of Rajasthan are famous in this respect throughout India. There is a sect of Jain sadhus called *Digambara* who literally "clothe themselves with the clouds", that is they go naked. They are allowed only a gourd for water and a peacock feather for dusting before they sit, in order to avoid squashing small creatures. They pull out all their bodily hair, using tweezers or fingers, after soaking the hair in an ash based compound. I met one of these Digambara sadhus in a Jain village. He was very insulting to me, and to all Hindu sadhus in general. He seemed an obnoxious, cantankerous old man whose penance had made him spiteful towards the world. He was also pretty nasty towards the Jains from the village who pandered reverently to his needs, as obliged by their religion. As far as I am concerned, if the result of undergoing spiritual rigors and austerity is to end up as an irritable old man, then I would rather be a luxury loving hedonist!

At first I did not have a very good opinion of the Jains, after my arrival in the Mysore area. Their religion seemed to me to be a somewhat narrow minded and fanatical version of Hinduism. However, I met and was looked after by several Jain families who gave me a feeling that my own opinion was biased by contact with a few bigots. Of any attitude to life of which I know, the Jain religion, seen in its true light, offers the most selfless and nonviolent approach.

CHAPTER EIGHT
The Ochre Robes

From Mysore I headed virtually straight back to Madras, as I was tiring of my circular South Indian pilgrimage and wanted to have some sort of base for a while. I had learnt from my friends the Subraminiya family in Madras of an ashram on the outskirts of the city at Tirumulaivayil that was run by an elderly sannyasin. This place turned out to be a haven for me for a month or so, and whilst staying there I made side trips into the countryside to visit two interesting holy men. These encounters remain in my memory, as both of them possessed interesting personalities. They were quite unique even by the standards of the Hindu spiritual world of sadhus and gurus.

Firstly I went by bus to a small village to see a holy man who had built up a reputation both in local villages and in Madras itself. This sage had devotees and visitors from all levels of society; farmers; teachers; politicians; and film stars. I found his abode quite easily as he lived on the open verandah of a simple house that faced a narrow main street of a village. Inside the tiny verandah he sat on a small platform at one end, with enough space for two or three people at the other. The regular flow of visitors had to queue in the street and shuffle forward to reach the verandah, where they could be within arms' reach of the holy man. A bus service ran right past the place and would stop outside to let some people off and to allow other passengers to make their obeisance with folded palms. Opposite the verandah, facing across the one lane street, was an open tent like construction where I sat down amongst other devotees and visitors to watch the proceedings.

The mahatma was dressed in a single dhoti and sat cross-legged on his platform, occasionally bending his head down to talk quietly to somebody in the queue. He looked very old, had matted hair that reached below his waist, and possessed very, very long nails. They curved in arcs and were each about a foot long: He sat with his hands resting on his knees, palms facing upward. Into these palms, visitors were placing offerings of rupee notes, pieces of fruit, or sweets. Two or three helpers who stood on the verandah were removing the offerings as they accumulated, and in the case of money, putting it into a square steel box. The fruit was pushed through a gap in the window which appeared to open onto a small room. Fruit was piled up high against the window and seemed to be filling up a large area of the room.

This I thought most peculiar as fruit rots easily in a hot climate. Even more fascinating, I found, were the cats. There were half a dozen of them wandering around, sitting on the swami's lap, and sometimes perching on his shoulder. There were several large bowls in front of him, and some of the visitors were bringing offerings of milk to tip into the bowls. Obviously the way to this guru's heart, in order to get his blessings, was to please his cats. The cats could also pop in and out of the gap in the window of the "fruit room" and I guessed that they at least kept the mice away.

The helpers on the verandah were obviously disciples as they regulated the queue, dealt with the offerings, (and the milk bowls), and, as became apparent, fed their guru by hand. They also put lighted cigarettes in his mouth and these were being proffered frequently by the seemingly poorer members from the queue of visitors. The swami would suck on each cigarette in one long continuous inhalation until it was half burned down. Then he would gulp before continuing with the rest of his smoke. Hardly any smoke would emerge from his mouth or nose, and I do not know what he did with it.

I found out more, because I spent a few days living in the open air structure across the road. Some of the chelas were happy to tell me the full story, as well as give me food and tea. Their guru had gone into samadhi trance over five years before and since then had only eaten what people fed him. Moreover, he sat in padmasan lotus posture permanently and did not wash himself, clean his teeth or clean anything. His body carried on while his mind went elsewhere. He defecated where he sat and, according to his disciples, had built up quite a "pile" around himself before people started looking after his physical cleanliness.

In the early days of his samadhi he was not recognized as a holy man and the local villagers would just give him a bit of food from time to time. Quickly however, he attracted devotees who began to wash, bath and feed him on a regular basis. Those helpers had moved him to his present spot and now, with all the money collected from donations, were beginning to build a small ashram. According to his loyal servers, the swami ate very little and his feces were never smelly, always giving off a pleasant odor.

    I noticed myself, whenever I went near him, that his body seemed to give off a somewhat sweet and sickly smell, not a disagreeable one however. The swami spoke rarely and then only in a quiet whisper. The devotees in the queue would ask him things and he would lean over and whisper something back. According to all that the visitors told me, he spoke in a very intelligent manner, in a soft voice. Even if he did not answer a question, he would listen intently and nod, or just flicker his eyelids. I went up to him several times and said that I was traveling round trying to improve my self-knowledge by meeting gurus and holy men. He always smiled at me and appeared to understand my English, (which I was told he knew). Apparently he gave instructions to his helpers that I was to be looked after while I stayed, as indeed I did for three days.

    I learnt that because the swami had been permanently in a cross-legged pose for several years, he was unable to unfold his legs. He did not seem inclined to move any way. Several times a day a curtain would be pulled across the tiny verandah and the disciples would take in water, towels and a fresh dhoti in order to perform their puja, by service of their guru. I also discovered that the accumulation of fruit in the small room did not rot, but dried out slowly. I presumed that the dry air and the enclosed space were preventing any decomposition. Most gifts of fruit and sweets in ashrams are redistributed as prasad to visitors.

Prasad is any food that has been offered to a holy person or to a deity in a temple, and thus has been consecrated. However, this particular swami's philosophy was that the donations of fruit contained the sins of the givers, which they were symbolically passing on. He did not want the sins to be redistributed and had ordered that all the fruit be deposited in that small room.

Several visitors from Madras spoke to me in English and told me that some very well-known and influential people would come here to try and receive the holy man's blessings. Usually they wanted to succeed in work, marriage, money, or some other materialistic area. In the West, a person with the swami's habits would be seen as a psychiatric case. However, he was in no way mentally feeble, the Hindu public does not flock to visit such. Do not think that it was all a gimmick either. The public was not gullible, but understood and appreciated the person whose mind had gone into the spiritual condition, rather than dementia. At that time though that sort of spirituality seemed to be a pointless if genuine realm, and I did not feel that his experience was the sort I was seeking. It just stirred up doubts in my mind about some spiritual goals.

I visited another intriguing and fascinating character. He had built a small ashram around a temple, which was situated on top of a hillock right next to the Madras/Bangalore road. A year before I went there, this hill top temple was a tiny, neglected shrine, with only the odd passer by bothering to climb up for darshan. It had a small, stone image depicting a form of Vishnu worshipped locally, and was reached by walking up a rough path to the hill top, which was about three hundred feet above the road. One of the local Brahmin caste villagers, who happened to be an electrician by trade, used to visit this temple from time to time on his way to or from work. He did not arrive home one night, and by next day all were out looking for him. Some of the villagers found him sitting in a trance state in the temple

The electrician could not be shaken from the trance state depths for several days, even though his wife, mother and family arrived quickly on the scene. He was left sitting in the temple. When he came out of his samadhi, he seemed transformed. For a start, he was unable to speak, and began to write what he had to say on paper, and later on a slate. He wrote down that he had seen the deity in person, and had been transfixed by the experience. Furthermore he said that he was staying at the temple, possibly forever:

Over the next few weeks this, by now ex electrician drifted in and out of deep trance states, hardly eating or sleeping. He used to have periods of deep breathing sounding like bellows, so powerful that people could hear him from the bottom of the hill.

    Villagers started to gather around the temple to see what was happening and in the following months, people from nearby began to regard this once family minded man as a holy soul. People brought him food at first and then helped him with his new found interest in the temple's renovation. The new guru announced that he was in direct communication with the temple god and had been ordered to make the place into a most beautiful and resplendent shrine. When I visited, the place was indeed being transformed into a palace.

    The simple stone idol was now clothed in gold and silver armor and festooned with jewels. Buildings had been erected around the temple to provide for visitors' needs and at the bottom of the hill large constructions were underway to accommodate kitchens and various living areas. I found the man who had started all this, sitting in the temple staring with sparkling eyes at the deity. A queue of visitors had lined up ready to meet him when he came out of the temple, and they were seated on a large carpet at the front. The yogi emerged, sat outside, and on his slate began to scribble answers and responses to his visitors' questions and requests. Often when asked a question, he would gaze in the deity's direction for a while before he "received" his answer, which he then passed back to the questioner. He explained that he received any power or ability through the temple god only. Powers indeed as the ever increasing flow of visitors proclaimed:

Most of the people coming to see him would ask for a specific blessing, such as promotion, wealth or fertility. The yogi "priced" each wish and put a figure in rupees on the slate! That was what the boon seekers had to give to the temple if they wanted the yogi's blessings. The money inflow was pretty high judging by the pace of development around the place. There were even, so I was told, plans afoot to build a school and orphanage after the temple works were finished. I thought that some of the devotees and visitors must have had their wishes granted by the yogi, otherwise his fame would not have spread so much. He was attracting a fairly large number of middle and upper class intelligent people, so he must have proved his powers or skills at some time.

This yogi in his schooldays had learnt quite good English, so I was able to communicate with him personally. I managed to get quite a bit of information from him as I spent several days on the hill top, by his invitation, as a guest. I said that I was intrigued by the "cash for blessings" system he operated, and that I thought it most unusual and perhaps not very spiritual. His (written) answer was that he only wanted to sit in the temple and serve his god, as instructed. The temple was to be made a beautiful haven for Hindu worshippers, and for that money was needed.

He did not want the money for himself. Indeed he slept on the ground in front of the temple and lived a very spartan life by any standards.

I was rather impressed by the yogi, and his continuing deep meditation periods, which he now regulated to hourly sessions twice a day. He seemed quite genuine in his devotion to the deity and he emanated joy and energy. He would bound up and down the hill during the day supervising the construction activities, using his chalk and slate to communicate. I was told that he used to be a skinny, weak person, but I saw that now he was well built and extremely fit. This was probably because he was engaged in manual building jobs. He appeared to have both physical strength and mental power as he leapt around the hill. Everyone followed him around as if he were a royal personage. I found myself feeling amazed at the circumstances of his divine awakening and subsequent change of personality, after all, he had been only an unknown electrician!

The village relatives and family of the new yogi had long ceased trying to draw him back into their fold, and treated him with the respect accorded to an accomplished holy man or guru. No doubt his wife and children had been through some hard times, but it seemed that they were now being drawn into a role in the temple as helpers and devotees. Personally, I was at times in awe of his very non - human presence. It did feel to me as if something very supernatural had taken over his mind and body.

I was interested in seeing if the yogi could impart anything in the way of spiritual knowledge or advice to me. He did not, however, seem interested in making disciples or being a guru in that sense and told me that he was unable to offer any advice or guidance. I felt that my contact with him was a valuable experience, but that I was not going to be able to emulate him in any respect. I decided that my search was not over and returned to Madras, to the ashram at Tirumulaivayil.

I spent a peaceful month or so in the ashram, which was known as the Vaishnavi shrine. The head of the place was a sannyasin who had been a distinguished lawyer in Madras. He spoke good English and was fairly unorthodox in his attitude to the spiritual life, by Brahmin standards. I spent a rather lazy time, wandering in the woods nearby or swimming in the tank, a large, deep man made pond lined with concrete. The water was reached by descending a couple of dozen steps, and apart from this access, the sides of the tank were vertical concrete. There are a lot of tanks in South India, mainly built for irrigation and water storage, but often taking on religious significance for bathing, especially when in temple grounds.

Hindus (except children) generally do not swim in their sacred tanks and rivers as this is deemed irreverent. Swimming is regarded as sacrilegious in such places because the act of bathing is seen as a dignified ritual as well as being cleansing. Sadhus especially are not supposed to set a bad example by indulging in cavorting, in holy water. I used to love to have a swim anywhere I could. Even in temple tanks I would have a surreptitious splash.

In the tank at the ashram, nobody bothered me and I used to spend hours there escaping from the heat.

One day whilst immersed in the tank, I saw a water snake swimming about. I did not worry about it too much, even though it was poisonous, and continued my soak. India is so full of snakes and other poisonous reptiles that I had long decided that I would accept their presence philosophically, like most Indians. After all, they had their life to live, just as I had mine. There were so many hazards to life in India, diseases, bites, food poisoning, bad drivers, and so forth that I felt it was useless to try to be a tourist who avoided contact with the environment. I wanted to live as the many millions of Indians did, and take my chances. On my travels I found it necessary to drink water from all sources, eat what I could get, and be in close proximity to the general public when crushed into a bus or train.

Generally the local transport was a rickety old bus that had seen better days. Seating for sixty meant that one hundred and twenty could be accommodated "comfortably-". The trains were just as bad (or worse), particularly in respect of third class coaches. The crush was often so bad that the only way into the carriage was through the window space. Sardines in a can, aptly describes the common standing room only situation, which favored the spread of various germs.

Vaishnavi shrine's grounds housed a number of wild animals, including foxes and mongooses.

I used to see mongooses in the evening on a path near my room, and watched them from the verandah. They were very playful, but quite cautious about human beings, disappearing instantly at the slightest noise. However, one small mongoose was very different. This one would wander around the temple area, especially when there were people sitting cross legged on the floor space in front of the temple deity. At the time of the evening temple puja, the sound of bells and gongs would bring out the tame mongoose, in search of a cosy human lap onto which to climb. New visitors to the temple often got a shock when this little furry bundle with sharp teeth popped onto their laps. This mongoose liked nothing better than having its tummy tickled, going into instant trance in the right hands.

One is supposed to have pure, clean hands, body and clothes when worshipping in a temple. Touching a cat or dog is impure, and mongooses are I think, in a similar category. As much as I liked playing with the friendly mongoose, it meant that I had to go and wash my hands before I could resume my seat in front of the temple. Some of the Brahmin worshippers were unhappy about this friendly animal being in the temple area, and would have liked to discourage it. However, the head swami, whose name was Parthasarathy, put about the story that this mongoose was a reincarnated sadhu, and thus there was little the pundits could do about removing it. I think this tale was swamiji's way of having a dig at zealous religious rigidity.

I began to call myself Swami Ram Prakash Ananda whilst staying at the Vaishnavi shrine. I felt that I was living the life of a sannyasin and should add the title (Swami) and the suffix (Ananda) to my name as is the normal procedure on initiation from brahmachari to sannyasin. In some ways I was being a bit egoistic. It is hard to explain, but there is a definite superior status accorded by the Hindu public to a sannyasin. Such status would make my life easier in terms of travel and staying in ashrams, as I would be shown a greater degree of deference and thus hospitality.

I discussed the matter with Swami Parthasarathy who sympathized with my decision to become a sannyasin without formal initiation. His attitude was refreshingly different from that of those who said I had to be initiated into the monk's life by a guru whom I had formally accepted. I had left, with bad feelings inside me, my last guru and had not met any swami or yogi whom I really wished to be my new teacher. I wanted to be own guide, for a while although I did not like to admit this, lest people thought I was beyond my level of spiritual attainment. (And this is generally considered to be a grave mistake). I probably did not want official, (and permanent), initiation for another reason. I still held the idea of returning to England at some stage, and probably I only wished to have the role of Hindu monk until I felt that my search for inner knowledge was completed. It was, for me, a means to an end, and not an end in itself,

To make the transition from brahmachari I had to change my white dhoti for the ochre or orange robes. I was going to dye them myself, but Swami Parthasarathy gave me, without any ceremony, a set of orange cloths. Many people, including sadhus of all types, were to be taken aback by my unorthodox entry into the order of swamis, but that did not have any adverse repercussions on me. There is a lot of in fighting and bickering amongst the various orders and sects of sadhus and sannyasins. Whether I was officially ordained or not, I would always come up against the criticism of followers of differing paths or gurus. What I actually found was that I could move freely between different sects and their temples and ashrams, simply because I was not particularly affiliated to any sect or guru.

I got a chance to belong temporarily to various groups of devotees and followers without hampering my non allegiance to any particular cause.

From Madras I planned to head north to Bombay and then to Gujerat State. My first stop, not far north, was at a village where one of the Shankaracharyas was staying. There were officially four such "bishops" in India, but this one was an extra fifth as he was recognized by the Brahmins of Tamil Nadu as being their particular head holy man. I did not think much of this elevated official of the Brahmin "church" as his only advice to me was that, as an Englishman, I was not qualified to go wandering around as a sannyasin. He said it was bad enough having many thousands of non-Brahmin sannyasins in India, but foreigners too - never: He told me that I should stick to Christianity.

He may have been right to a degree, but as I had never considered myself a Christian his words did not seem very helpful. Incidentally, in North India, many consider over the Shankaracharyas as pompous, and they have little hold over a lot of sannyasin sects there. I found later that the few sannyasins initiated directly by the Shankaracharyas from Brahmin castes were usually extremely erudite in Sanskrit and religious laws. Sadly many of them seemed bigoted and cantankerous.

After my brief encounter with the Tamil guru, I wandered on towards the holiest of all shrines in South India, Tirupati in Andra Pradesh. While on this section of my travels, I reflected on my lifestyle and tried to evaluate what I was doing. For a start I was living very simply. I was barefoot, possessed a few orange cloths, a towel, and a cotton shoulder bag. I had no watch and could not remember when I last had one. I did not worry about the lack of a timepiece, as in India it was not a necessity. Unless I had a train to catch, it was quite sufficient to go by the sun, and by dawn and dusk. My spiritual quest was proceeding apace in terms of searching out the answers in the exterior world of gurus, holy men and temples.

However, my inner quest had lapsed. I no longer sat in meditation, turned my beads, or even read much in the way of scriptural material. I could sit quietly for long periods at a time doing nothing, but often I was bored and waiting for the next meal or cup of tea. The boredom I felt impelled me to keep wandering in the search for the elusive Sat Guru. I was unable to settle down to the practice of proper sadhana. It was a vicious circle because my wandering only increased my restlessness and in reality pushed me farther from the spiritual path. I wanted at times to abandon the whole quest and return to the West. However, I had sunk even deeper into the sannyasin role, and did not wish at that stage to suddenly admit failure.

Apart from the recurrent wish to leave India, I did not know how I could change things practically. I had no means of raising the money for my fare out, and to ask to be repatriated by the British High Commission would have been a humiliating mental defeat. I had not contacted my parents since my arrival in India and I was unwilling to have to face them after ignoring them for so many years. People continue in roles that they do not fully want to be in for years, before they suddenly make the change, prompted by a nagging subconscious.

For instance, a person will stay in a marriage unwillingly for the sake of children, or other reasons which are kept on a prominent mental level. Then one day something snaps and he or she takes off into the blue. That point for me was some years away still.

Although I continued my travels and spiritual search, I was developing a, growing feeling that there was perhaps nothing to look for in the first place.

Without the continuing travels though, I would not have gained the experiences and insights that brought me gradually to my final conclusions. My brief encounter with the Shankaracharya just north of Madras had triggered off a period doubts about continuing my travels as a sadhu. However, I decided to keep going as far as Bombay at least, and then review the situation. For me, the next two stops generated even more questions about Hinduism and holy men, but I did find them educational experiences.

Tirupati, the most holy of shrines in South India, is situated on a plateau at the top of a mountain. Huge numbers of people visit, many going up the five mile road by bus. I walked up, taking the steps, and actually made the journey at night time, with a short sleep on the path side.

This is one temple where foreigners (or rather, non-Hindus) were definitely not admitted, and there was even a policeman on duty at the bottom of the steps to check people. In the darkness however, I managed to get by, and in the morning duly took my place in the massive, slow moving queue for darshan of the deity. People in the queue took me for a native of Kashmir, where they have fair skins, and because I was in sannyasin robes, I was told to go straight to the front of the line of several hundred pilgrims.

There was a separate small line for the temple's V.I.P. guests, and sannyasins and holy men. Having been ushered straight into the temple, and told of the millions of rupees worth of jewels adorning the idol, I managed to have a very brief darshan of Tirupati*, (a form of Vishnu). I felt crushed by the milling throng inside and, to my great relief, got out quickly.

*Tirupati - from Tripati, a Sanskrit word. (Pati=lord of the three worlds).

After my temple visit I sat down nearby to talk to some sadhus of the Vaishnava sect. Whilst sitting there I heard some loudspeaker announcements (in Telegu, and was told that they were asking people to be on the lookout for foreigners and to report them to the manager's office. I was approached by a man in spotless white cloths who said he was from the manager's office.

He asked me where I was from and, on hearing, said I would have to furnish documentary proof of my Hinduism if I wished to enter the temple. When I told him that I would not bother as I had no proof, he asked me, apologetically, to return soon on the bus. He said that I was welcome to a prasad lunch packet free, and went and brought me rice, etc. wrapped in banana leaves. When he came back, he also gave me the money for the bus ticket. Thus I had my meal, free bus ride, and darshan at the Tirupati temple, although I saw the idol so briefly that I have not the vaguest memory of what it looked like.

In most of North India, all this business would have been considered laughable. I had found that a sadhu there is considered a Hindu whatever country he comes from In South India however, orthodox Brahmins still have strict control over the temples, and consider anyone from outside India to be unclean, as they do many fellow Indians. In many ways, I was glad to be heading north out of the non-Hindi speaking areas. In the North, I could walk into any temple and be welcomed as a sannyasin or a sadhu, with honor. Apart from some fanaticism though, I had found South India to be full of warm and friendly people, some of whom had kept me alive!

In the State of Andra Pradesh, a Hindu saint of some world-wide renown had his headquarters. This was Satya Sai Baba who appeared in his pictures dressed in long, bright red kaftans, sporting a bushy, Afro type hairstyle. I had read and heard quite a lot about this modern guru, mainly how he cured the ill, and materialized all sorts of items from his empty hands. He was well known for the production of ash from his empty palms. He was said to be able to produce this ash at will from his clenched palms, and even his photographs were said to produce droppings of ash around them. I had also heard not so flattering stories also. To have a look for myself, I turned up at the ashram where I found myself in the midst of a throng of visitors and devotees, all-waiting for darshan of the holy man.

Everyone seemed to be milling around aimlessly, not knowing, when or if they would get to see the great man. I found a European guy who showed me rooms where some Western disciples were staying, but he told me that everyone was left to fend for himself or herself.

I did not stop long at the SatyaSai Baba ashram. As soon as I arrived there, I was turning myself around preparing to go on my way. Some people do need miracles, but then I wanted to find a peaceful place where the culture of ancient India was offered as a far better richness than any amount of material wealth. I have found myself desiring miracles. Had I gone there at a different time I could have had a vastly different experience. It was not to be at that time

My next stop further up the railway line towards Bombay was at a place called Mantralayam still in Andra Pradesh. I had been told of a large temple there, which was built around the Samadhi of a saint who had died some hundred years before. Burial in a state of samadhi is quite often taken by advanced yogis on a predetermined day. The "ordinary" Hindu is cremated to release the soul, which goes to heaven or hell for a while prior to rebirth. The souls of self-realized mahatmas do not go anywhere as they have attained a liberated state, but their aura remains in the Samadhi where they are busied

The Samadhi shrine is treated as any other holy temple in India and puja and all the accompanying rituals are performed there. On the anniversary day of the yogi's samadhi, a special puja is performed, for which, at the most popular shrines; there can be a turn-out of thousands of worshippers.

Mantralayam is literally a "place of mantras" shrine. I discovered it was a huge place visited by thousands of pilgrims each year. The saint and yogi whose body is interred there is said to have left notice that he would remain in a trance state for four hundred years, during which time he would be "available" to visiting pilgrims. The reputation that had grown up around his shrine was that any pilgrim making lengthy circumbulations of it would be rewarded by darshan of the saint in their dreams. The saint would then grant favors and dispense blessing so that the pilgrim's desired benefit could be obtained.

People would come to spend days walking round and round the Samadhi so that they could achieve religious merit for the after world. More often, however, they wanted to fulfill a material wish, promotion, examination success, childbirth, wealth etc. Walking around any religious site in India is considered a meritorious deed, and must always be done in a clockwise direction, so that the "pure" right hand side faces inwards. This is a *parikrama*, and can be round a temple, just the inner shrine, or even around a whole village area that has sacred connections.

The inner shrine at Mantralayam was enclosed by a large covered outer walkway which made all weather *parikrama* possible. Public donation had enabled the building of a large number of rooms, which were available for the use of pilgrims. Many pious Hindus give money for building such accommodation called *dharmashalas*, ("houses of dharma"). Dharma is an all-encompassing word for sacred law, act or duty. A few devotees lived permanently at the shrine and spent their lives looking after the flow of pilgrims. I was made most welcome for the few days I stayed. I listened to many tales about pilgrims who had seen the "resident" saint in their dreams and who had received guidance and blessing this way.

Quite a few of the visitors spent periods of fasting and meditating, and even without a physical guru in residence, the shrine was a peaceful spiritual haven. I found the place uplifting and not influenced by the usual ritual activities and commercialism that one often finds at important Hindu temples. There were no Brahmin pujaris who charged a scale of fees for various official pujas to the deity. Neither was there a resident swami or guru with a flock of followers.

I left Mantralayam in a bullock cart from the shrine to the railway station a few miles distant. I could have walked there more quickly and comfortably but a group of village farmers, whom I had met at the shrine, insisted on taking me this way. They were simple people from a place some fifty miles away, and they had been intrigued by my way of life and nationality. They had taken pains to look after me at the shrine, bringing me sweet delicacies and endless cups of tea and milk. They spent a lot of time listening to the story of my travels and telling me about their life and what Mantralayam meant to them.

I was very impressed by their sincerity and devotion to their traditional Hindu beliefs. They seemed untouched by the goings on of the political and material world, and were content if they got a reasonable crop each year. They insisted on buying me a ticket for my next stage, and said they hoped that the punya of my future visits to holy places would rub off on them. I felt that even if was not going anywhere holy, these people would have insisted on helping a traveler like me on his way.

Many Hindus I met helped me because I was a sadhu and they believed in serving such people. However it was more than that. Devout Hindus were very proud and pleased when they saw that a foreigner had adopted their own beliefs, practices and religion. That I had become a sannyasin as well made me even more honorable and respected in their eyes.

So much is made of progress and materialistic achievements in India today, and yet there are still millions who believe that we are born to use our life for spiritual, not material, purposes. That I adopted their own ideals, was often firstly a surprise, and then a source of great pleasure for some devout Hindus. They could then point to the cynical and materialistic amongst them and say, "look, even people from the West are beginning to appreciate our culture and spiritual values".

So many Hindus that I met seemed genuinely appreciative of my lifestyle, and moreover were often concerned that I should not have to undergo too many hardships. I was finding that in my role as an orange robed English sadhu, the necessities of food and shelter were no longer a problem. There were many occasions when hospitality, respect and friendliness were showered on me to the extent that I felt overwhelmed.

For my part, I tried not to disappoint people, and endeavored to be as genuine a spiritual searcher as I could. I began to identify more positively with my role as a wandering monk and forgot about returning to England for a while. As I moved back northwards, I returned to the use of Hindi. As I met very few Europeans in this period especially in the village areas. As I was beginning to speak reasonably fluent Hindi, I began to find myself being asked to give an hour's talk in the villages or towns where I stayed. Along the Narmada river it was often a case of speaking before a dozen or so people in someone's home or a village hall. As well as this, I was approached by schoolteachers and invited to give talks before their assembled school children.

If I visited a school, they would gather everyone, teachers and pupils, suspending classes in order to listen to a talk about my experiences and my beliefs as a Hindu sadhu. For a small village in many areas, the arrival of a European sannyasin was quite an event, especially when I spoke their languages and had developed a fairly interesting speaking style. I became quite confident in public speaking and took to giving talks to larger and larger audiences. My morale at this time concerning my adopted lifestyle was climbing high and I enjoyed my new found prestige.

The lecture circuit in North India is big business for some educated swamis. In many big towns and cities, interested people will organize events housed in big tents, inviting perhaps twenty speakers for the week, fortnight or even month. The organization, advertising, and funding for these events is usually very good, with speakers being invited well in advance, and their travel and accommodation needs met. With thousands of listeners in the audience each day, the speakers receive a reasonable "purse", as the income from donations during the events can be high. Some of the swamis who have a good popular speaking style travel the country, giving lectures for a large part of the year. They can become quite wealthy, and build large ashrams, housing dozens of "ordinary" sannyasins.

CHAPTER NINE
More Holy Men

Getting nearer to Bombay I passed into Maharastra where the language is Marathi, one of the North Indian languages grouped along with Hindi.

I had left behind the Dravidian part of India and latterly the language of Telegu which is spoken in Andra Pradesh. Although Hindi and Marathi are from the same group of languages they are as alike as German and English. Hindi is widely spoken in North India but it can be difficult for a Hindi speaker to understand the dialects of other states. Gujerati, Marathi, Hindi, Urdu, Punjabi. Oriya, Bengali, these are the main languages without considering the states east of Calcutta. Language was never a problem for me in India, as I always found people willing to communicate at some level, whether by sign language, through an interpreter, or using a mixture of languages. Hindi, however, was widely known and used in the North.

Whilst in Maharastra I visited a mountain top ashram some miles out of Satara town. It is very common in India to find pilgrimage places; temples and sadhus' dwellings built miles up from the nearest human habitation on any suitable hill or mountain top. Quite a few such places are four or five miles from the nearest road, with access by track or, in the more popular places, by thousands of stone and concrete steps. Some of the stone stairways, ascending into the heavens are very old and must have needed an enormous amount of human labor for their construction. In the smaller of such places, one finds at the top a temple, with often a few sadhus in residence, and perhaps some simple shelter for the pilgrim visitor. Everything except water in these elevated retreats is brought up on human backs, and thus the diet of those who live there is kept very simple.

In spite of the poverty and isolation of such retreats, I was invariably offered something to eat and drink after walking up for perhaps four or five hours. I might get plain roti with a little chilli chutney, washed down with lemon tea. Mountaintops in mid India are lovely places to visit after enduring the heat of the plains. It is only in the Himalayas that they get snow and very cold weather. The more Southern ranges have a lovely warm climate with cool breezes in summer. Pure water is always one of the amenities available in these places, usually from a spring. Often a few lemon trees and some vegetables and herbs can be grown to provide a little variety in the diet. There is such a difference when one descends to the heat, squalor and congestion of the bustling bazaars.

I found Bombay to be a shock to my system after staying in so many lovely secluded places. However, I had the address of an ashram set in the hills behind the northern outer suburbs. Not two miles from the hustle and bustle of the Bombay suburb Borivli, there began expanse of hilly forest and jungle. There, at the end of an isolated road were situated the Kanheri caves. They had been hewn out many hundreds of years ago by Buddhist monks, when they had a major sway over India. It had become a picnic spot and tourist haunt at weekends, when buses ran from Borivli up the winding forest road. I walked to the caves mid-week, sweltering under the hot sun.

    The sun shines harshly most of the time in virtually all of India except when it rains for a few months of the year. It can be hot during the winter in Bombay, and uncomfortably so in Madras. In summer just about everywhere it was a murderous, vicious heat with which I had to contend. Thus it was that about five months after leaving Dehra Dun in the winter, I was plodding barefoot up the scorching six mile road to Kanheri

    Kanheri caves were set in a hill overlooking a stream, and nearby were views down across the forest to Bombay. Such a contrast to the grime and bustle of Bombay and yet so near. Beyond the caves on a small lush plateau was the rock cave home of a well-known sannyasin who had spent many years resident there. He had lived ten years in the area, mostly under an individual large rock, in which there was a natural cave like shelter. For five of those years there had been no motorable road and people only visited the place on forest department business.

They still had wild tigers roaming around there, just miles from one of the largest cities in the world. The swami's rock home itself had been the home of a tiger until he took over the premises. The land around the rock had been transformed into an orchard of fruit trees, mangoes, plantains and grapefruit. A fine new small temple had been built and the swami now had several cows, plus a bull which wandered at will in the forest. The cave overhang of the rock had been altered into a comfortable room with a sliding partition. At the front, a verandah had been built and at the side there was a kitchen.

For the first few years .The swami had spent his time living wild in the forest, living on roots, berries and herbs. There is a root, known to ascetic yogis, in the form of a large tuber that provides a filling meal and keeps away hunger for days on end. The swami lived here alone in the beginning except, that is for the tigers and monkeys who did not seem to mind a human companion.

After a few years of solitary living in the jungle, our recluse was discovered by some devout followers, who then began to make the long trek out to visit him bringing food, seeds and tools. After five years, one devotee came to stay, becoming a disciple.

This *chota* swami, or "small" swami, was still there when I arrived, serving his guru and managing the ashram that had developed. He too had become a sannyasin and had been there for five years. He had enlarged the cave for his guru with the help of devotees from Bombay, who gradually increased in numbers. Years on and the place was a splendid retreat with food and shelter for any visitor who wished to stay a few days. It was still very peaceful and quiet except for weekends, when some visitors to the Kanheri caves would come across to the temple, and numbers of devotees would arrive in order to spend a day with the two swamis. The devotees would bring provisions and cook a large meal. By sunset on Sunday however, the last visitors would depart on the buses and all would return to tranquility.

It may sound as if the swami was quite a recluse and ascetic, or at least had been. There was more to it than that though, as he had been performing a penance over all those years. It was a physical penance that is still practiced by a few in India. All the ten years he had spent in the forest area, he had remained standing. Except for the last year, he had stood throughout the night, sleeping by supporting himself on a chest level swing. He had two ropes suspended from the roof of the rock, and joined to these was a plank of wood, making a cradle for leaning on with his hands and arms.

His legs were swollen to four times their normal size and were a reddish blue color. Only after much pleading by his followers and devotees had he recently agreed to lie down at night. At the time I stayed there he spent the whole day standing at his swing, taking only a few short walks to the temple or to the grounds. As well as standing all those years, he also observed a vow of *mouna,* or silence, during the day.

Why torture oneself? It is an accepted means, according to Hindu scriptural lore, of purifying oneself. This tapas is performed in a variety of ways for many different reasons. Variations include standing, holding an arm in the air, sitting between wood fires in the scorching sun, or living naked in the cold of the Himalayas. Perhaps better known in the West is the fakir with his bed of nails, the butt of many jokes. The reasons for performing tapas in India range from a desire to impress the public in order to make money, to the wish to purify oneself of sins and to attain God. With the swami, I can only suggest that he felt the need to cleanse himself of either something from the past, or from some aspect of his personality. I was told that prior to his leaving home and family, he had suffered a disastrous love affair. More information than that was not divulged.

I spent a couple of weeks at the Kanheri ashram and visited another sadhu who had built a place some two miles further into the jungle. It was quite a trek to this other spot, especially for someone carrying supplies. Yet I found a very cosy wooden building housing the sadhu and a few followers. He was a chillum- smoking type with long, matted hair and a rather ferocious appearance. However, he was friendly enough and made me welcome for the day I spent there. It was a beautiful, but isolated, place and yet this sadhu must have had some following in the city because his little ashram had been well appointed and provisioned.

I also had the occasion to meet one of the local tigers. They frequented the caves area, especially at night after the visitors had gone, and were in the habit of snooping around the swami's cow sheds, where the cows were locked up at night. The swami had kept some dogs in the past but they had been carried away by the tigers. The same had happened to dogs kept by the forest ranger who looked after the caves and lived a mile away down the hill.

The swamis did not seem afraid of the tigers and they would shout at them or chase them if they caught them prowling around. I suppose after so many years of close contact, there was some sort of rapport that stopped the tigers turning on the swamis - or their guests like me. One evening a few devotees and I were sitting around a small wood fire outside the cave, next to the kitchen door. We heard a loud crackling sound coming from nearby bushes, just as if someone wearing boots was approaching and crunching leaves underfoot.

I was quite surprised to be told that this was a tiger, as I thought that they moved silently. I was told to sit quietly while the younger swami got his torch. He moved just into the kitchen with the intention of playing hide and seek, as the tiger was coming to snoop around. I jumped out of the kitchen doorway behind the swami with his torch, and surprised the tiger "in the act". The swami chased the tiger a little way while I followed, until the tiger turned and gave out a shattering roar. I fled back into the kitchen, quivering with fright. I could still hear the swami's shouting, interspersed with a few of the tiger's mighty roars. I knew that the two mahatmas were a bit fed up with the tigers' designs on their cows, but I did not know that they had such a dialogue with their neighbors. The tiger vanished into the trees to join a mate and the roars of the two of them reverberated in the surroundings for some time.

    I was quite scared as I was sleeping at night on the open verandah. However, I was told that the tigers would not molest any sadhus and, in spite of some roars from the surrounding hills, I got a good night's sleep. I think that there was some cordiality between the swamis and the tigers, and this was confirmed a few days later. Two hunters came to a nearby cave one night and staked out a goat with the intention of luring a tiger into range of their guns. The two resident swamis were very angry at these hunters and during the night banged pots and pans and shouted in the hunters' direction. The tigers stayed away and the goat lived another day too.

    I was told that the land on which the ashram had been developed belonged to local government through the agency of the Forestry Department. High authorities had decided it would make an ideal place for a tourist complex Thus an inspector from some department arrived one day and told the swamis of plans to remove the ashram, and that the spot would possibly include a deluxe hotel, and they were going to be evicted. The official also nailed up notices to this effect. The inspector had a heart attack and died the day after he had been to the ashram. Following this, no more was heard from local government officials. Word then filtered back to the swamis that certain pious Hindu officials had also taken up the matter, and were saying that the ashram was on sacred ground.

I could not verify the truth of the story, but I do know that there are a lot of officials in high places in India, who are devoted to the Hindu cause in general, and to the welfare of holy men in particular. Quite often, gurus and sadhus with property problems get things sorted out by their devotees. Their followers could include lawyers, government officials and police officers, all of whom would be willing to make efforts on their guru's behalf. People and places that have religious significance in India can often circumnavigate local laws or other difficulties and regulations

I experienced the red - tape of Indian bureaucracy myself on occasions. I found quite often that because of my foreign "visitor" plus sadhu status, friendly officials would help me side step the rules. Usually the more senior an official one got to know the better, as a mere word from such a person could expedite things on the spot. Complicated forms in quadruplicate could then, in India, be dealt with in minutes. All that is required of the ordinary person is a money "gift". From the holy, blessings will suffice. A lot of official systems in India have been constructed, out of proportion to necessity, behind a façade of paper work. However, virtually anything, even medical degrees, could be obtained for the right amount of money.

Corruption is common in many countries of the world. In some it is the norm, and India is no better or worse in this respect than many other Eastern countries. Anything can be, and is, done in order to supplement the meager salaries and low standards of living found in such places. I heard of cement for dams and bridges being adulterated to increase the bulk. This makes extra for illegal resale. Contractors often need to do this to recoup the money already spent on "buying" the contract. The list of foods that can be adulterated is long. Milk, flour, sugar, rice, and cooking oil, these are a few products that can be added to for profit. It is of course an unhealthy aspect of life in more ways than one. People even get used to the fact that the things they consume or use are impure or flawed. Thus villagers brewing illicit liquor will add a dose of fertilizer, or the insides of batteries to their brew to add flavor and potency: One can read in the Indian newspapers of incidents where fifty people die from poisoned alcohol in one village, or twenty from bad cooking oil in another.

Death from various easily preventable causes was thus not uncommon in India, and is a state of affairs that caused anger and embarrassment to many honest citizens. Strong efforts are made by successive governments to reduce corruption but the situation never seems to get better. It is one of the deep rooted problems that make India a difficult country to love for all her aspects. On one hand there is such wealth of spirituality and the allegiance to profound philosophical values. On the other, one cannot avoid the realities of poverty, squalor, corruption and top heavy, bureaucracy. The last at least is a legacy of the British Raj, and whilst the British built roads, railways and bridges, they made little impression in some areas and created problems in other. Politicians and leaders in India are faced with an overwhelming task. They have my sympathy whatever course they choose to plot.

I left the Kanheri ashram after a pleasant stay, having made good friends with the two swamis. They gave me the address of a sadhu who was a *mahant*, the head man, of a sect of Naga (naked) sannyasins. Such sadhus in former times used to be recruited from warrior castes, form armies of ash smeared ascetics, and fight on the side of kings who supported religious causes. When there was no special cause to battle for, different groups of these Nagas would fight amongst themselves. In spite of their outwardly primitive appearance these sadhus lived in *akardas*, (ashrams for Naga sadhus), which were often very wealthy establishments.

They used to keep elephants and store a variety of regalia and furniture for mainly ceremonial purposes. They possessed vast tracts of land and thus had an income to provide for their needs. The mahants of the better endowed akardas used to live like feudal lords, with their small army and elephants. These mahants would dress up in finery and live in a luxurious, and sometimes sensuous, manner. Their sadhu band of followers had to behave and dress differently of course, like good ascetics.

The Naga sect with its mahants still survives in India as they have retained in some places a bit of land. Generally the mahants have received their title to the property from their guru, who has chosen them to hold the purse strings as well as the authority. Although this sect attracts or has attracted the less educated and lower castes, I found that the mahants were often intelligent sannyasins who were trying to change the image of their sect.

Quite a difficult image to lay down considering the Nagas' history. Many of the sect today still keep some of their traditions such as nakedness or semi nakedness, ganja use, trident carrying, and the general wild man appearance. To some they are seen as anti-social and, although they are treated with respect as holy men, they are regarded by some as inferior to the educated and clothed swamis. There are still sizeable numbers of adherents who follow the centuries old traditional way and like to keep their individual fakir type image.

The mahant I was going to visit had a place north of Bombay at Tryambak. This is a village, overlooked by surrounding mountains and containing an important Shiva temple. First I had to travel on the main road to Nasik, and then catch a local bus for Tryambak which was ten miles or so away at the end of a country road, through the foothills. Beyond lay the barrier of steep sided mountains, which cut off Maharastra from the coastal strip of Gujerat. To one side of the village was a hill called Nila Giri (Blue Mountain), where there was a long flight of concrete and stone steps leading to a plateau.

Up there were small temples, a few wooden buildings and the home of Mahant Swami Siva Giri Maharaja with his smell band of sadhu disciples. Shiva Giri, (literally Shiva Mountain), was a jovial, plumpish witty and talkative character. Although not a well-educated person, he was knowledgeable in the path of yoga. He was a sannyasin with ochre robes, although his real affiliation was to the Naga sect. He did not smoke ganja (although some of his disciples did), but I found out later that he enjoyed a drop of rum on certain occasions. He owned some land, which he had "inherited" from his guru, the previous mahant of this akarda. He was also building a house in the village, where he seemed to have developed a close relationship with a female devotee. The sect of Giri sadhus, who all have this "surname", have an offshoot called Goswamis who are married. I noticed that getting married from that particular brand of sannyasins was not all that unusual.

The name "Giri" is quite common in India, apart from its use by sadhus. A recent President of India was a Giri. Shiva Giri gave me the nickname "London Giri" and began to call me that at all times. As I stayed at his akarda over the rainy season, this name came to be the one I was known by in Tryambak. Informally at least I was an honorary initiate into a Naga sect:

Ganja played a large part in the life of many of the less erudite Naga sadhus. For them, its use is perhaps similar to the use of cannabis by Rastafarians. Ganja is used in a chillum, and smoked to the accompaniment of chants and hymns to propitiate the god Shiva. The chillum has to be inhaled on in one long, controlled blast, until flames shoot out from the top. The higher the flame, the more one's standing amongst sadhu chillum smokers. Despite modern public opinion, (and law) in India, people generally accepted the Naga sadhu's way of life.

The devout often brought these holy men their dope, just as they would make an offering in a temple. On certain sacred days a huge ceremonial chillum would be put into use and passed around, with even essentially non users accepting a puff. For a devotee, the offer of a sadhu's chillum was something of an honor and I saw that even police and other officials who visited the akarda would have a lung full on occasions. After many years of not smoking, I tried the chillum again, but I found that my lungs had become sensitized to smoke, and I politely declined further offers.

As I spent the last months of the rainy season at Nila Giri, I was able to learn a lot more about the traditions and practice of the sadhu's life in India. Shiva Giri was an encyclopedia of such knowledge and was always eager to talk at length on such a subject to any interested audience. One of the pieces of information I gleaned concerned an ashram near Bombay. I was told that this particular place was massive both in building and garden space. It had been designed and constructed on most modern lines by a very interesting swami who had filled the place with foreign disciples. I resolved to visit this ashram one day and see if I could sample some of its modern amenities. I was getting too accustomed to bathing by a spring and using the woods for a toilet, and I wanted to remind myself of how Western people lived, spoke, and thought.

My immediate intention, as soon as the rains had ceased, was to cross the Western Ghats to Gujerat State. Many sadhus regarded Gujerat as a land of "milk and honey" because the Hindu population there was so devoted to holy men (and women) of all types. Besides being well known for their business and commercial abilities, Gujeratis were renowned to sadhus for their hospitality and rich vegetarian cooking. Sadhus traveling or living in Gujerat reported that they received a lot of respect and were well looked after in every respect.

My first impression of the Gujerati people was very favorable. To go over the mountains from Nasik, I had to catch a bus to Bulsar, (a largish town on the Gujerat coast). Mahant Shiva Giri gave me as a departing gift some rupees to cover the expected cost of the whole day bus journey. However, I found out at the ticket desk in Nasik that my twelve rupees was quite a bit short of the required eighteen rupees. A couple of Gujerati men standing behind me stepped forward and insisted on buying me the ticket, even though I was about to purchase one for half the journey. "Maharaj", one of them said, "We cannot let you travel around Gujerat like a pauper". At the midday stop at the top pass in the middle of the mountains, I was invited by my newfound devotees to join them in the restaurant for lunch. I had a very well presented vegetarian thali, (tray of food) and was treated to tea, fruit and sweets at further stops in the afternoon on the way to Bulsar.

Throughout my stay in Gujerat, I was to find myself the recipient of generous hospitality in large doses. I found this a change from South India, where I had often gone hungry. Here the problem was to be looking after my health. Owing to constant invitations to meals which turned out to be feasts, I developed a few problems. Lots of ghee,
sugar and spices make up the base for various Gujerati dishes, which include vegetable curries, *kheer* (sweet rice pudding) and mango juice desserts. I found that such a "diet" was not beneficial for my system, especially in such a hot climate.

Too much sugar, hot spices and oily food are not conducive to good health. I had been eating plain fare for eons, it seemed, and I found the chance to indulge in "tasty grub" irresistible. I stuffed myself for my first few months in Gujerat, until I began to feel the side effects. I started to suffer from "prickly heat". And lots of rashes erupted all over my skin, causing me to rage at the excruciating itchy torture.

Tea is drunk more frequently in Gujerat than anywhere else in India. The two to three cups a day average of many Indians seemed to become a ten a day custom in Gujerat. Tea means a concoction made of tea leaves, much sugar, and milk, all boiled together in a saucepan for ten minutes.

The result is a sickly but strong brew, of which I became a "devotee" for quite a while, until I discovered the effects of it on my system. I came to realize that Gujeratis seem to suffer a high rate of Western illnesses. Diabetes, heart ailments and cancer seemed to be quite common. I am not criticizing the Gujeratis. It is just that, like the French, they love their food.

Arriving at Bulsar in the evening I thanked my benefactors and headed off to the local sannyasins ashram, where I was made welcome and spent a couple of days. There I received several names and addresses of places to visit along the Narmada River, which passes by Baroach. I traveled north to Baroach and the Narmada, and then spent some time wandering along the sacred banks.

The Narmada is a very holy river to Hindus, and to some it is the equal of the Ganges. One of the pious deeds to be performed there, especially for sadhus, is the *parikrama* pilgrimage. Starting at the estuary mouth one has to walk to the source and then back: down the other bank to the mouth again. Many sadhus do this pilgrimage and spend a year or two in the process. Studded along the banks are temples, shelters and also small ashrams of the holy men who have decided to settle permanently. The hamlets along the way seemed geared to the passing "trade" of pilgrims, and many villagers are eager to meet new sadhus, hear their stories, and provide them with food and shelter.

Although marriage and raising a family is the norm in India, one meets many householders, especially in certain areas, who seem to spend nearly all their time in the temple or in the company of sadhus. This applies equally to both sexes. Men or women may have their traditional duties to perform, but if either starts spending a lot of time in ashrams and temples, they are not really open to criticism in such a devout country. Often one finds a whole family with strong religious leanings, and they always seem to have some swami or sadhu staying as a guest.

I felt that religion brought a lot of "color" into the lives of many Hindus, who did not then have televisions, pubs, or the diversions and amusements to the extent of Western society. Many create for themselves a good social life through involvement in temple *bhajans,* (songs of praise and prayer), and ashram satsangs. When it comes to participation in religious ceremonies, there is an opportunity for men and women to be equally involved. It is very difficult though for women to take up the sadhu or sannyasin's role, although there are some well-known female gurus who have a large following. Usually they have had their devotees and ashrams from the beginning of their "career" and have not spent time as wandering ascetics.

Generally speaking, India then had a society that revolved around the male. They get the jobs, the money, and rule the family set-up. The wife is often a servant of her husband, and women on the whole lived life doing menial tasks, even if they were well educated.

Modern education trends have made some change and given many women more intellectual possibilities and some practical independence too. However, shortage of jobs and the low standard of living means that many degree holding women remained as housewives doing the cooking and cleaning. Life is hard in India for many woman, but then it is not particularly easy for the man either. The need to provide falls on the male shoulders - and that, in India, can be a very grim task.

Religion offers a vital outlet for both men and women who seek solace from their worries through their association with holy men. Temple worship and other ritual provide a diversion from daily drudgery. Many women go to hear religious discourses, which provide for them a welcome break from the responsibilities and routine of the home. They also get together with other women for a good chat, and generally use the occasion for social purposes. India needs its "opium of the masses".

When a swami or sadhu of some erudition or intellectual capability visits a village, he will often be invited to give a talk or lecture to an assembly of interested locals. This will take often take place in a temple, hall, during the evening when people are freer.

There are many halls in India specifically built for the purpose of satsang and bhajan, and even small towns will have these places. A swami or pundit may be invited to spend a few weeks giving regular discourses and attract a large lay public following. In order to be "big names" on the lecture circuit, they have to be able to quote a good range of scriptural excerpts - both in Sanskrit and regional languages. They have to blend a mixture of the devotional works of the popular Ramayana and Manhabharata, with interesting presentations of the drier philosophical works. Some of them are very good at their "job", and I quite envy their oratory skills.

Though in parts poverty stricken, India is not shortcoming when dealing with temples and holy men. Some of the temples and ashrams have had millions of rupees spent on them. One could say this is money better spent on improving the lot of the poor masses. With that view, a state with no religion at all would be an efficient ideal for which to aim. One should remember of course, that most countries do tend to spend many millions on armaments and so forth depriving the poor just the same. The rich remain rich and the poor remain poor, but neither seem to really wish to escape from the strong religious influence on their daily lives.

I do not think that the majority of Indians seriously want to undermine their religion. Hinduism (and India) can seem pretty crazy and illogical to outsiders, who only see the logic of their societies. India remains strongly individualistic because Indians seem to accept both overpowering religious and cultural mores as well as materialism and even Communism, (as some States vote Communist).

When I stayed on the banks of the Narmada, the river level was back to normal, following the rainy season. Near the river mouth under the bridge at Baroch the river was a mere trickle as they had received little rain that year in the catchments areas. Upstream there were ford-able stretches and then miles of wide, deep pools that had to be crossed by ferries.

The banks in places rose up hundreds of feet from the river, and were there deeply undercut by the rainy season's surges. Villages on the top of such banks were literally toppling in the water, all due to changes of flow direction during the monsoon season floods. The year before I arrived, they had experienced a devastating flood when the river rose fifty or more feet in places and washed away several villages.

Hundreds had died, and I heard many tales of miraculous escapes, combined with the story of the brutal toll.

Floods are not unusual anywhere in India during the rainy season. All rivers are subject to incredible level rises and in swollen conditions they often change direction, flooding different areas each year. I visited one orchard on the Narmada that had been inundated by the previous year's flood. The family living there had survived on their roof tops for several days, and all the crops and animals had been lost. Luckily those people lived, and the water had brought rich silt down, which would provide soil fertility for the future.

Large-scale catastrophes are common to India. In one wet season a natural dam burst high in the Himalayas near Badrinath. The road up from Rishikesh has a heavy flow of bus traffic, taking pilgrims up to the sacred source of the Ganges. On this road, that clings to the mountains above the Ganges gorge, a dozen or so buses were held up in darkness by a landslide. At the same time a dam burst high up in the mountains. This released a surge of millions of gallons of water into the river, the level of which rose up to where the buses were waiting, with disastrous consequences. All the buses were washed away and the death toll was high. Still, despite flood hazards, people living on the banks of rivers like the Narmada, remain in villages that could slide into the river.

Where else can they go? They have little or no alternative. There is limited provision in a poor country for those poor who suffer from natural disasters. They were poor to begin with, they are poorer after disasters.

In spite of their problems, I found the village folk of the Narmada region to be a happy, hospitable people, and I thoroughly enjoyed a month in their company whilst visiting the numerous temples and sadhu residences. After that, I decided to head back to Bombay en-route for Maharastra in order to see some more places in which I was interested. I wanted to go as far as the Ajanta and Ellora caves and. then return south to visit the ashram of Swami Muktananda. He was the guru about whom I had heard so much, the swami with the big, modern ashram and the large following of Western devotees.

CHAPTER TEN
The Sat Guru

The time I chose to return towards Bombay was inauspicious. A civil war had been raging in East Pakistan for some time and it looked as if India and Pakistan were going to war soon. I found that during international conflict involving India, foreigners can suddenly find that life becomes rather tense. In a very volatile country some people tend to harbor paranoid feelings concerning other countries and their nationals, even in times of peace. Much of this suspicious attitude has been directed towards American intentions, or rather towards "C.I.A. infiltration", spies supposedly being active as Pakistani agents The problem is that any white skinned person can be regarded as a "C.I.A. spy" when paranoia is exacerbated by international conflict, especially when America is not taking the Indian side. There are many in non-affluent countries that harbor a deep seated resentment or suspicion towards Western countries and their nationals.

The foreigner in India is often the object of distrust due partly to the general lack of knowledge (concerning world politics), of the poorly educated. Some politicians promulgate this tendency by paranoiac assertions in public, although I am not sure whether this is deliberate or due to the state of their political abilities. When a war or conflict occurs involving India, a foreigner can become suspect, and those who have become sadhus are doubly suspect. I have heard stories from Indians about various "spies" dressed as sadhus being caught near army camps, and found to be working for Pakistan. I only heard such tales when there was some political tension. Generally, however, sadhus and holy men do not receive such untoward attention, and indeed have devotees amongst the top brass of military, police and political bodies. I also heard, from foreign travelers, tales of unfortunate incidents where they were in the wrong place at the wrong time and perhaps took a photograph that got them shot at or arrested. In peaceful times the highest Indian official may gladly show you around restricted premises if you are a foreign guest. At times of conflict you could almost get lynched for walking across an insignificant bridge, or for a photograph of an innocent railway engine.

  Violent public outbursts in India are directed in a very intense and often random fashion. If the public decides that a certain sector of the community is culpable, then anyone having a connection with that sector is possibly in dire danger. When the Chinese invaded India in 1962, Chinese businesses that had been established for years in India were attacked. When Indira Gandhi was assassinated by Sikh gunmen in

1985, Hindu youths and others went on the rampage and slaughtered over a thousand innocent Sikhs. Neighboring Pakistan has a similar temperament. When Americans were accused of involvement in the seizure of the Mecca shrine, a well-organized mob attacked the U.S. embassy in Islamabad and razed it to the ground.

This time when I traveled down to Bombay on the train, I felt that people were looking at me differently. One chap started asking me if I had been to Pakistan, and what I thought of the place. Nearing Bombay, police searched the train, and I was asked by one of them to get off the train for questioning. However, I remembered my British passport, pulled it out of my bag, and thrust it at the policeman. The policeman seemed surprised and, without looking inside the passport, returned it after telling me to stay on the train. When I looked at my fellow passengers I got the feeling that they thought that I had just produced some sort of Indian secret service identity card. They did not get a chance to see that my document was just a passport and now instead of being a possible Pakistani spy, I must be an Indian spy. It did not seem to make them any more friendly or chatty and in fact they all became utterly silent - unusual for Indian railway travelers.

Continuing my journey in Maharastra, after passing through Bombay, I found that the atmosphere of war had become very thick and that people seemed cool towards me. Several came up and asked me outright if I was a spy. They told me that they assumed I was one as if it was the most natural thing in the world to be. I could have told them I was indeed a foreign agent and their Indian politeness would probably have led them to offer me a cup of tea: Until they dashed into the nearest police station that is. This all happened at the time when America was brandishing and parading a fleet off East Pakistan, as if to threaten India intervention there. Feelings against Americans, and thus any English speaking white person, were very high at that time. Later I was to meet several European travelers who told me of the hassles they had experienced during that period.

    Threatening crowds on railway platforms or in the bazaars were the most commons occurrences.
When war did break out between India and Pakistan, I stopped my journey towards the Ajanta and Ellora caves, and took refuge in a quiet ashram in the heart of rural countryside. The war was short, and within weeks India emerged happily victorious, along with the formation of Bangladesh. I was then able to breathe freely and wander forth at will. I went to the nearby town of Aurangabad to say hello to Mahant Shiva Giri as I had heard that he was staying at one of his devotee's houses there. I had the address of this devotee - a local politician, since I had met him in Tryambak previously. I stayed with Shiva Giri and his politician followers for a few days, and discovered that Shiva Giri was well liked by these influential people partly because he shared their rum: Alcohol consumption is considered a deadly sin amongst "proper" Hindus, although then quite a few of the wealthy class

indulged. Having a guru who fully condoned their behavior must have been very congenial to these semi Westernized politicians. I had a bad cold at that time and was persuaded to have some rum; my first alcohol for over five years. It did my cold the world of good. However, that was the only time I was offered alcohol during the whole of my ten year Indian sojourn.

Most vegetarian Indian families have no dealing, whatsoever with alcohol, and it is considered very base behavior for a sadhu to drink, although ganja is acceptable. Many states in India were "dry", alcohol being illegal. Bootlegging was fairly common, especially among some castes, villagers and also the non-religious in the cities. Brahmin drinkers were rare, whilst some "warrior" caste men take to whisky like ducks to water, when they choose to drink. The Bania or Vaishya castes of shopkeepers and traders are usually very orthodox and strict about what they consume. There are many Vaishnava sect followers of these latter castes who consider than even the use of onions or garlic is debased, as they are believed to excite the senses. India with foreign expertise, produced its own beer and rum, but much of the alcohol available to the masses was of the home brewed variety, often a harmful and sometimes lethal concoction.

I did not miss alcohol at all in India, because its unavailability to me put me completely out of the picture. I quite liked alcohol. However, I realized that a totally alcohol free life was not a problem to come to terms with, and that gave me a good feeling. The difficulty I later found was in being able to participate in stimulating pleasures in a moderate way, so that one does not suffer the disastrous effects of over indulgence. A high rate of dependence on alcohol, drugs, cigarettes and coffee, is a price of an affluent society, where we have and enjoy. If India was suddenly to become as rich as America, then I just do not know how much religion would retain its hold over the average impoverished Indian.

Up until now, since leaving my first guru, I had been searching for the teacher and path that would seem right for me. I wanted to feel that I had arrived on a spiritual plateau where I had full access to the inner guiding light. I had become half aware in terms of self-knowledge, but I felt unable to live my life as effectively as I wished. The next step after my aborted foray in the direction of Ajanta was to return towards Bombay in order to visit the ashram of Swami Muktananda at Ganesh Puri. I had been hearing a lot about this place and of the wealthy guru and large contingent of overseas followers living there.

Right from the start I could tell that this ashram was going to be unlike anything I had experienced so far in India. I got off the bus outside a long, ornate, concrete and marble building which had impressive temple domes at each end. It was surrounded by a high wall, and stretched alongside a narrow country lane that led only to the village called Ganesh Puri. A sparse, barren and hilly Maharastran landscape spread out in all directions, giving the place the effect of being an oasis in the desert. The scene was lent more impact by the fair skinned people milling about outside. The men were wearing sadhu type dhotis in bright orange, red and maroon hues, topped with Day-Glo colored shirts. The women had equally bright saris or robes of similar colors. Many sported silk or wool hats, and quite a few of the men had shaved heads. The whole initial effect of this ashram and its inmates was somewhat surreal. To me it was like arriving at the gates of heaven after traveling through the wilderness. The place was made more impressive by the lush gardens and orchards, which spread out into the distance behind the other ashram buildings of which I had seen only a part during my approach by bus.

    Set into the middle of the high wall was a large, ornate archway. There were devotee helpers in attendance at the gate, directing the regular flow of visitors to one end of the courtyard where there was a many tiered rack for shoes, which was supervised by another ashram resident. From the marbled courtyard one could walk barefoot into the large, central prayer hall which contained, at one end, the shrine and life size marble statue of the deceased guru, Swami Nityananda. Everything here was of the best materials and looked both sparklingly modern and pleasing in design. The whole ashram, as well as the village of Ganesh Puri, had developed around Swami Nityananda, who had been the guru of Swami Muktananda.

Having received spiritual powers and abilities from his master, Swami Muktananda had dedicated both the temple and his yoga method to him. Swami Nityananda had been acknowledged as a *Siddha*, a perfect soul - by the thousands of pilgrims who had poured into Ganesh Puri for his darshan when he was alive. They still came in droves both to visit his rooms at Ganesh Puri, and his now more widely known disciple, Swami Muktananda and his new ashram.

Swami Nityananda had possessed a huge, corpulent figure and spent his time reclining on a couch dressed only in a loincloth. He was considered to be a *Jivan Mukta*. (Enlightened saint). Devotees and pilgrims would file past him quietly paying their obeisance's to receive his touch, which alone was reputed to be capable of bestowing great spiritual awakening. One such visitor who arrived to stay and serve his new found master was the forty year old Swami Muktananda. He had been wandering the length and breadth of India for years, searching for a perfect guru who would guide him to true self-knowledge. Swami Muktananda received a powerful blessing from Swami Nityananda, and was then told by him to go away, meditate, and achieve final perfection through Siddha Yoga. Siddha Yoga is the way to self-realization through worship of, and adherence to, the teachings of the perfect, or Siddha Guru. It requires the follower to depend upon the process called *Shakti-paat*, where the guru bestows the necessary grace. Shakti-paat awakens the disciple's kundalini shakti; the sleeping "serpent power" coiled at the base of the spine.

After ten or so years of vigorous sadhana, Swami Muktananda returned to Ganesh Puri, acknowledged to have become a Siddha. On the death of Swami Nityananda he took up his guru's mantle of spiritual power. Although his style was very different from that of his master, he began to attract a large following from all over the world. In his mid-fifties, he took to wearing bright, silky clothes, multi colored hats, and a variety of sunglasses. He traveled to Australia, Britain and America opening or creating Siddha Yoga centers wherever he went. He did not speak English or teach anything other than that concerning Siddha Yoga, the path to self-knowledge and connected aspects of the Hindu tradition. All his teachings and speeches were translated from Hindi. As the disciples and devotees from all over the world began flocking, so Swami Muktananda started giving out the brightly colored hats and shirts that were his own trademark. The ashram and its facilities grew at a rapid pace to accommodate the American and European disciples who wished to stay a few weeks or months. It became very popular also with the growing number of Bombay and Maharastran devotees.

They inundated the ashram at weekends, arriving in the special buses that had been laid on from Bombay.

When I entered the ashram, I was very impressed by the buildings architecture and the facilities for the hundreds of residents. The gardens were a magnificent haven for those who wished to sit quietly and meditate. Further behind the ashram were orchards, farm land, and cow sheds, all managed and looked after by the resident disciples. There were a few bungalows, built by affluent Indian devotees, who wished to spend their spare time with their guru. The properties were rather like holiday or second homes, although these were not here for beaches or ski fields.

There was even a purpose built elephant house where one lively elephant was kept. This elephant had two full time mahouts, (keepers), and was paraded daily in the marbled courtyard outside Babaji's quarters. The elephant was painted and adorned with silks for this ceremonial occasion, and Babaji would feed it fruit and buns before an adoring crowd.

The whole place with its showcase trendiest did seem a bit bizarre at first to me. I had not seen anything like it during my stay in India. I had not been to, an ashram where hundreds of foreign disciples were wandering about, especially ones clad in sadhu type robes. In spite of my skepticism, I was interested in Swami Muktananda's teachings as, to date, I had not come across a mahatma who was so clear in his advocacy of the Siddha Yoga path to awaken the Kundalini Shakti.

When awakened, this serpent power eventually reaches the center or chakra situated at the crown of the head. The result is supposedly mukti, a freedom or liberation which is the same as nirvana, Zen awakening, or self-realization.

I knew that the awakening of Kundalini could be accompanied by various physical effects, resulting in aspirants going into different trance states, or breaking into bouts of spontaneous dance like movements, (like the whirling and twisting of dervishes). I had read that other effects could occur, like the seeing of bright lights or the hearing of inner music. Personally I was doubtful, not only of Kundalini, but also of Swami Muktananda's professed power to awaken it in all and sundry.
I was told I could stay at the ashram as long as I liked by Swami Muktananda's ashram manager, an ex-businessman who had wide control over everyday matters. Everyone who stayed at the ashram was expected to do some sort of work, and I found that even as a sannyasin I was not exempt from this rule. Work meant spending a few hours each day wherever one was allocated, and this could mean gardening, toilet cleaning, office work, bookshop duties, or guiding visitors around.
*Babaji - Swami Mluktananda was known by this term of endearment and respect.

I had not been accustomed to any sort of job or routine other than that of my own choice since I left the Dehra Dun ashram. Since then my experience was that swamis and sadhus were not expected to do any sort of manual work, and I had become used to a rather lazy life. However, as I wished to find out whether Swami Muktananda had anything that would benefit me, I decided to stay and accept whatever tasks were put my way. I also wanted to know why Babaji had so many followers who displayed such intense devotion. I wished to find out what his powers were and what his attraction was.

Swami Muktananda had already made his first world tour before my arrival and had established centres in Australia, America and Britain. Owing to this recent tour there was, at the time of my stay, an expanding number of more than a hundred foreign devotees of both sexes living in the ashram. There were dormitory type facilities for both men and women. There were also a dozen or so permanent Indian disciples in residence, all holding the more major supervisory type jobs in the temple, the gardens, the office, or in Babaji's personal service. Everyone, including the weekend guests, participated in the same basic daily programme. This meant a few hours work, bhajans for two hours, and an evening session of half an hour or so in the prayer hall. People were also encouraged to use the underground meditation rooms, which had plush satin cushions and upholstery, and to attend Babaii's afternoon lectures. One was, however, free after attending the evening and morning prayers and doing a few hours work.

It was not a rigidly organized place, except for the morning and evening, sessions, and anyway these were on traditional Hindu lines and customary in most ashrams. A lot of devotees spent their spare time sitting or standing around the special seat in the leafy courtyard where Babaii sat from time to time during the day.

I found out very quickly that Swami Muktananda was a very powerful guru. He sat cross legged on his seat, sometimes jovial, sometimes fierce looking, but always emanating a kind of radiance. He looked at people with a penetrating gaze that seemed to be searching out unfathomable depths. I saw why he attracted so many. His presence and gaze were hypnotic. For all the outwardly playful, bubbling personality, one got the feeling that he was the wielder of some power and that he had been to a place where few had trodden. I found his aura almost frightening at times. I felt that he must have some of the same sort of power that creates presidents, dictators, popes, saints, and military giants like Napoleon or Alexander. I found it unnerving how his personal Shakti would draw devotees to stand around him all day, just staring and taking in his presence.

Babaji was in his sixties when I visited, but he looked much younger, and indeed attracted even young or teenage children of his Indian devotees. He sat, a slightly plumpish figure seemingly like a temple idol come to life, with his sparkling eyes and translucent complexion. I had no doubt about his abilities to attract any type of person from any position when I saw the effect he had on both his followers and casual visitors.

Many people in the morning and evening hymn chanting sessions would get up and move their bodies in rhythmical dance motions whilst in trance like states. In meditation anywhere in the ashram people would start to roll their torsos and heads around or start to inhale and exhale ferociously. Mass hypnosis? Perhaps? The atmosphere of the ashram seemed to have an almost drug like effect, and it certainly began to affect me after a few weeks.

I was given plant watering as my job at first, but as I had knowledge of Indian languages, I soon became a helper at the main entrance, and began to guide groups of Indian visitors around the ashram. I quite enjoyed my role and found that I had quite a coveted post. I could take a group of, say, Maharastran villagers, around and show them the gardens, the plush meditation chambers, the temple and Babaji's courtyard and platform seat where he gave darshan. I had plenty of contact with ordinary day visitors and was thus able to remain somewhat aloof from the mass of disciples whom I still felt were over entranced by Swami Muktananda. They seemed so dependent on him, right down to their very reason for existence. This was in spite of the fact that Swami Muktananda preached repeatedly that the true self within is unique - find it and you yourself will be a Siddha and your own guru. In this respect Babaji was always very self-effacing, pointing out that as the Sat Guru is within each individual, the external guru is only needed to guide one to this source. I wondered why, if his disciples were truly following his teachings, they were so subservient to his person, like faithful pets.

In spite of my feelings about many of Babaji's devotees, I too began to experience trance like states during my meditation and bhajan sessions in the ashram. I began to sway about and then get up and dance in an introspective, blissful mood. However, I rarely went to Babaji's lectures nor did I go for darshan when Babaji was sitting in the courtyard. In fact I avoided him and tried to get on with doing my own thing, which *was finding the guru within*. I felt that I was getting the full benefit of whatever spiritual energy was floating around the ashram, even though I did very much as I wished with my spare time.

I found that I began to lose a lot of the lethargy that had been building up since I stopped doing sadhana and started traveling. I started going, to sleep at 9 p.m. and getting up at 2.a.m. in order to meditate for three hours before the morning communal session. I could go into meditation very easily whilst in the special underground rooms, and I attained there a deep and profound stillness of my mind. At the same time I felt that generally I had more mental clarity than I had known before. In spite of the dramatic and positive effect the ashram was having on me, I still felt that I had little in common with the majority of disciples and followers of Babaji. I believed that I was getting somewhere spiritually without having to wander around and behave like one of the flock.

I started to have some rather vivid and colorful dreams. In one I had a vision of Swami Muktananda resplendent in a gold braided Admiral's uniform. The ground was swaying beneath me and, having given a salute, I toppled over. I woke up in a sweat, but was not displeased with my dream because the colors and light effects had been magnificent. In another dream I found myself standing next to the shoe rack area just inside the main gate. I felt dizzy and collapsed slowly onto the pile of shoes. I seemed to be heading into a dark tunnel as if my life energy was draining away and I was being sucked into the nether worlds. Suddenly there was an explosion of light and I saw Swami Muktananda resplendent in gorgeous silk robes, sitting on a jeweled throne. Again I awoke abruptly a sweat, feeling very shaken but exhilarated. I thought that death might bring something like the experience I had just had, and that if I was going to end up in an explosion of light it would be a, joyful experience.

I felt very serene after my second dream and walked around for days thinking that death would be an ultimately pleasant "happening". I had begun to experience some peace and clearness of mind, and felt that Babaji was perhaps guiding me on an inner level. I still did not ask questions or seek his advice like most of his devotees, as I felt even more that the real Sat Guru would guide me on a mental level, without the constant physical contacts. From what I experienced, I began to accept that Swami Mulaananda was able to guide and direct me without the verbal contact.

Although I was not a worshipper of the physical Muktananda, or a disciple follower, I began to feel that he was a Siddha and a Sat Guru.

I stayed at the ashram or ten months and only on three occasions went up to Babaji and asked for some advice. The first time was due to finding that various mantras kept popping up in my mind and turning themselves over and over in seemingly automatic repetition. When I approached Babaji about this he said that the inner Shakti contained all mantras, and the awakening of this as Kundalini was causing the up rise and outflow of them all. Siddhas, he said, had knowledge spontaneously of all mantras and their uses. He recommended that if I was in any doubt about any japa (repetition) of a mantra, then I should repeat Om Guru Om.
Om (or Aum) is *the* sacred word of Hinduism and is a mantra itself.

It was also one into which I had been initiated in Dehra Dun. It is composed of A, U, and M in terms of sound and refers to the creation, sustenance and destruction of the universe. It also refers to the inner self, (Atma), in conjunction with the outer cosmic consciousness, (Brahma). The word Guru itself is used as a mantra because it is composed of two meaningful sound parts. Gu means "darkness" and ru "to remove". Thus the literal meaning of Guru is "dispeller of darkness".
As well as giving me a mantra, Babaji gave me a new name. He had heard that I had been named London Giri by Mahant Shiva Giri sometime before and he told me that he knew Shiva

Giri well. However, he said he thought the use of London with Giri was not very appropriate and suggested that I have a proper all Indian name. He told me that I should call myself Ganesh Giri, after Ganesh Puri, the name of the local village. Ganesh is actually the elephant form god in Hinduism, and is worshipped as the "remover of all obstacles". I was quite happy to use this new name and dropped completely my previous Ram Prakash Ananda with its memories of Dehra Dun. From then on, Ganesh Giri was my name in India.

    On another occasion when I spoke to Swami Muktananda I was thinking about leaving, but was not sure what I was going to do next. I asked Babaji if he thought I would be doing the right thing if I continued my wanderings. He said that if I was not sure what to do next, I should stay for a while in the ashram until I had decided what I wanted to do. He then went on to tell me that I was English and I would always be an Englishman whatever I decided to do. He felt that there would be no problem if I wanted to return to England and resume whatever life I chose, as my spiritual status would be unaffected, as it was unnecessary for me to be either a sadhu or a Hindu. He said that I would probably tire of being an Indian sadhu after a while. I was not at this stage thinking about returning to the West, but now I began to consider seriously again the pros and cons of it. I had been in India six years and, although I had not quite done all that I wanted to, I knew then in the back of my mind that I was going back "home" at some not too distant moment.

Eventually I decided to leave Ganesh Puri with; I felt, a higher degree of self-realization and a better approach to spiritual life. I wanted to find out if I had really changed through my contact with Swami Muktananda. I also wished to know if I had the ability to be a guru of others in India, and hoped to find some place to set up my own small ashram. I was not interested now in wandering in search of a guru. That, I felt, had been achieved and put behind me. However, owing to my insatiable curiosity, I was still interested in meeting other "famous" holy men, if only to see how they compared.

Swami Muktananda 1972

Swami Muktananda's Ashram
(Siddha Yoga Dham)

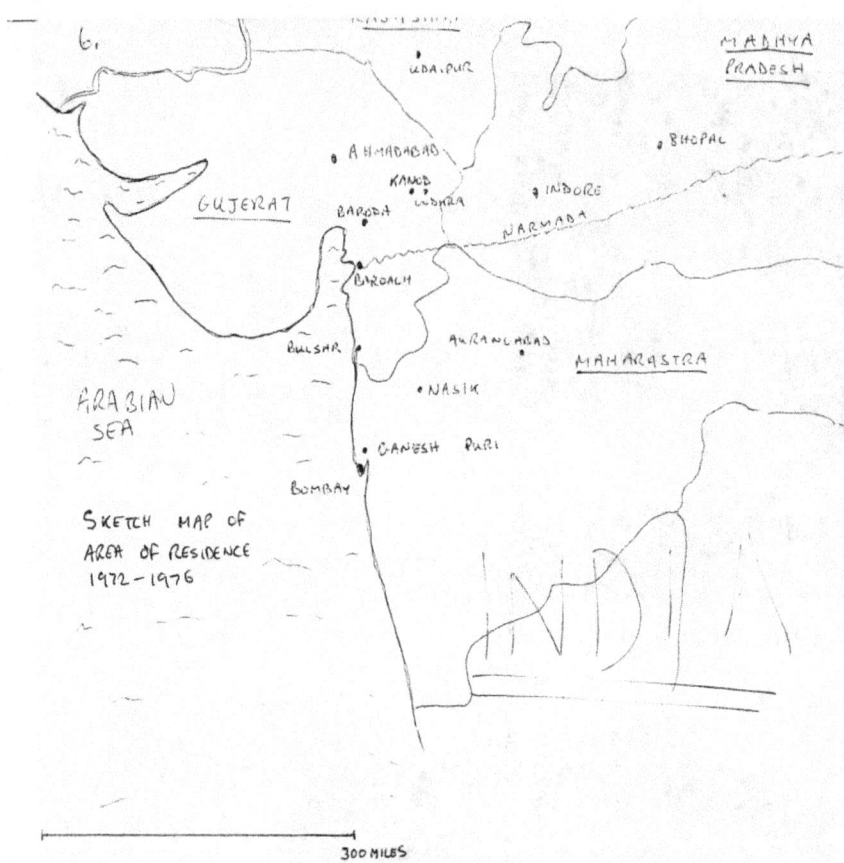

CHAPTER ELEVEN
New Home

I had arrived in Ganesh Puri in December 1971- It was not until autumn 1972 that I set off on my travels once more. I wanted to find a place where I could settle down for a while. My first move was not, however, to the countryside but into the big city of Bombay. Bombay has a large number of ashrams and I managed to spend the whole winter staying in a variety of them. I just passed the time quietly whilst continuing with some meditation and yoga. I took one trip to the outskirts of Bombay in the Poona direction, because I wanted to visit a camp that had been set up by Rajaneesh and his followers. He was another Indian guru who had "tamed" the West, and was initiating thousands of foreigners into his own variety of sannyas. I had heard that he was a professor of psychology, wore white robes, and rejected much of the traditional and orthodox teaching of other Hindu gurus. His followers wore orange pyjama suits and carried his picture in a locket on a rosary around their necks. One other very prominent aspect about him and his followers was the cult of free love that they professed which of course attracted a lot of attention in such a strictly moral country as India.

I found Rajaneesh's camp to be sparsely populated by orange clad people who appeared to wandering aimlessly. I discovered that there was a charge for the food provided as well as for "ticket" to Rajaneesh's lectures. This was something I was unaccustomed to finding in India, and I felt shocked at the time that business should have been juxtaposed with religion. Perhaps they were not selling religion anyway, but rather a new way of life or culture. Whatever was on offer, I found the atmosphere at the camp to be a bit empty. I did not have the means either to purchase a meal there, or buy the lecture ticket, which I thought exorbitantly priced anyway. I wandered away to the town and the samadhi shrine of a Sindhi* saint, where I was made welcome by some Sindhis who helped look after the place.

*Sindi - now part of Pakistan. There are a lot of Hindu Sindhis in Mumbai.

Rajaneesh Archarya (teacher) went on to become Rajaneesh Bhagavan, (Lord). He moved to America, setting up a huge, ranch like ashram, and of course he made a lot of money. I did not keep up with the details but he became good material for newspaper and magazine articles mainly, it seems, on account of his eighty white Rolls Royce's and five large airplanes. I felt quite jealous really as my progress as a budding guru never even bought me a bicycle!

Whilst in Bombay I visited a large temple and ashram complex under construction, which belonged to the Hari

Krishna group. This seemed to be inhabited totally by Westerners, and I found that they took their particular type of Hinduism very seriously. I went to a meeting at a devotee's house, where their world-traveling guru was to be in attendance. I had darshan of their guru and found him to be a pleasant, but very stern looking elderly man. I think that because I had half adopted sannyas and held my own brand of Hindu belief, I was regarded somewhat suspiciously. I thought that they saw me as some kind of infiltrator, who wished to convert them from their sole devotion to Krishna to a wider or different view of Hinduism.

After living in a number of areas in what was then called Bombay, I realised that I would never be happy in such a big city, and that if I was going to find a place for myself, I should head for a country area. I was getting bored with living; in ashrams established by other people, and felt that until I had my own place, I could not get to grips with a nagging question. Was I really Ganesh Giri, a Hindu holy man, and should I settle down to a life of devotion to this role? Or was I Raymond Pattison, with a totally different lifestyle and. destiny awaiting me in England? I did not wish to give up the sadhu life if I could be a successful Hindu guru. For all my spiritual progress, I had more ego than I had possessed before I started my sadhana in India!

It is in fact well documented in yogic scriptures that when a person starts to attain any degree of progress in sadhana, he or she can be sidetracked very easily towards social and material benefits. My desire at that stage was not so much for money, but for social power. Hindu teachings explain that according to the laws of karma*, people with great power and money have attained that position by their struggles or penances in previous lives.

*Karma - a Sanskrit word literally meaning "action".

It is that effort which produces good and bad "rewards", i.e. high and low births, heaven and hell. If the fruit of those endeavors is used wisely, then one can rise to a high level. If not used wisely, then any powers or pleasure accrued is enjoyed, and thus dissipated. This can lead to a downfall and, according to Hindu gurus I have met, this fact is illustrated in the lives of some famous, or rather infamous, people. People like Hitler, for instance, would have done some great penance in past lives, but on account of self-centered interest have been re born into a life where they have misused their karmic rewards. Once the fruit of good deeds is exhausted then a person falls from whatever high position had been achieved, the descent is usually rapid. According to karmic philosophy, people who have done good deeds and who desire sensual pleasure will find themselves enjoying a place amongst the angels until it is time to be re born. A spiritually minded person, however, who does good deeds and curbs the desire for rewards will not go on to heaven, but will be reborn indefinitely into a suitable environment for further spiritual progress. This process continues until final and full self-realization is attained when the cycle of birth and rebirth is destroyed due to the absence of any self-centered desire.

Over the next few years I did not attempt to change whatever destiny had been ordained by my own karma. I did not try very hard to assert myself as a guru of others, (in spite of my inner desires). I found that I was not attracting a following of any size. Eventually I came to the conclusion that my destiny lay elsewhere, and I was even not meant to be a Hindu. Perhaps this was for the best, as my motivation contained a lot of self-interest. In the light of karmic rules, had I become at all powerful, I would have lost the benefit of my years of sacrifice and endeavor. However, I did go on to have, at least in a very small way, an ashram of my own.

I do not know why I spent so long in Bombay when did not think much of that city as a place to stay. Looking back I realize that subconsciously I still wanted to depart the shores of India for England. Bombay the Gateway to India also represented the gateway out of India for me. I feel that I spent my winter there hanging around hoping that some act of destiny would materialize and whisk me away. When my time had not arrived, I decided to move to the area of the Narmada river in Gujerat, that had been my favorite place to stay. So I left Bombay without being fully aware of the number of months that had just passed.

I still did not have a watch, or any superfluous possessions, although I had taken to wearing sandals again, after encountering the thorn strewn paths on my previous visit to the Narmada banks. I had ceased to wear plain drab colored ochre robes as Swami Muktananda had given me some silk dhotis and shirts in a bright orange color. 1 rather liked my new image and decided to keep this rather non ascetic look. From then on I always wore bright colored silk dhotis and kept them in place with an orange plastic belt which had a solid silver buckle: Apart from the "trendy" sadhu outfit though, I maintained my simple style of travel with the small shoulder bag. I never had to worry about bedding, because firstly India is usually too hot to need any, and secondly, wherever I went, I could always find a mat and a blanket if necessary. I was completely accustomed to sleeping on a hard surface with only a mat underneath, although if I stayed in someone's house they would usually want me to have a mattress. Mosquitoes did not seem to bother me much and anyway my usual top sheet of a spare dhoti provided surprisingly good cover when stretched from toes to neck.

 Since my arrival at Ganesh Puri I had found that my body had become very sensitive to the food I ate. Up until that time, I could enjoy, in moderation, any food that came my way, including sweets, milk, products and spicy curries. Now I found that even small quantities of tea, sugar, or chilies were giving me skin rashes. Also if I ate any milk products or oily food I developed indigestion and then a cold. I began to try to eat very plain fare, such as rotis without ghee, and boiled vegetables without any seasoning. This was not always easy as I was often dependent on getting food as available, when given to me by a household or in an ashram. Whenever I visited a village in Gujerat I would invariably get several invitations to houses for meals. The food prepared would always be rich in spices and oils, as Gujeratis love to feed their guest the best food they can. It is, of course, a good excuse for them to have a feast too. My request for plain food would often disappoint people as they felt embarrassed to offer a sadhu guest plain roti and dhal. It also made them feel guilty if they were having gourmet cuisine while I dined simply. I did find, though, that people respected my ideal and need for a simple diet to a large extent, and friendly Hindu families would often go out of their way to cater for me especially.

    I spent the spring and summer of 1973 wandering all over a large area to the north of the Narmada. I was getting to know a lot of people in that region, with the consequence that some "devotees" were looking around their own village localities in order to find a suitable spot for me to settle down. Many towns and villages have some sort of accommodation for passing sadhus - often a hut built next to a temple. The devout Hindu locals felt that such a facility is a necessity in accordance with their religious decrees, and hope that a yogi or mahatma of some ability will come to live in their vicinity. The devout person would then be only too happy to visit such a sadhu and make sure that all the supplies needed for his upkeep are kept flowing smoothly.

There is often some competition between Hindu villages to see who can build the best temple or attract the most interesting holy man.

It is very easy to assume that the type of Hindu who is always running around visiting temples and sadhus has a very simple mentality. Nothing could be further from the truth. It is the educated and the wealthy who see to the finance and upkeep of temples and ashrams. Some huge new temple complexes have been built by India's richest families, and some of the highest - placed public figures have been prominent in promoting certain gurus and sannyasin causes. The poor and uneducated in India are perhaps as much superstitious as they are religious, and do not always support the full orthodox Hindu tradition. It is the middle and upper classes that compose the main body of support for sadhus and sannyasins especially in terms of monetary assistance. Quite a few millionaires have sannyasin gurus, and supply them unflinchingly when funds are required to build a new temple or expand an ashram. Of course the advent of the flood of Western devotees who followed world traveling Indian gurus, money, poured into some establishments on an incredible scale. That new activity was however, confined to a few gurus and the great proportion of support for Hindu culture was still very indigenous.

What of the poor then? Why is it that all this money is spent on temples and holy men, instead of on alleviating the misery of India's millions of destitute and poverty stricken?

The Hindu philosophy or outlook on life. Is that if one gives to a holy cause, i.e. a, person or place having religious merit, one accrues punya towards a place in heaven or a healthy next life. Thus by the observance of this very fixed rule, the big temples and their Brahmin priests get richer, and the well-known gurus and spiritual teachers build bigger palaces for themselves and their followers. If one gives to the poor or destitute, the gift is limited and given after performing: other duties such as feeding Brahmins, sadhus, or by Hindu scriptural decrees. One can feed pundits and leave some scraps for the poor. One can build temples and Sanskrit colleges, leaving a few books for some local orphanage. Anything else does not result in the rewards of a wonderful after life.

Many in India, including politicians, have tried to tackle the prejudices and practices of Hindu casteism and the blind following of religious observance. The aim of providing a better life for the poor and downtrodden can also be flaunted widely and publicly by a variety of do-gooders, who do not always have other peoples' welfare as their priority. There -are so many obstacles to change put up by Hindu beliefs and practices and yet it is the "correct" thing to do to show public concern over the plight of the poor. New Indian laws against caste discrimination were not effective in practice, because in spite of "modern" ideas, the influential Hindus still follow closely the ancient traditions. Otherwise they would not be true Hindus or at least they would feel they were going against their spiritual preceptors' injunctions.

Some areas of India have made progress in providing a fairer allotment of wealth to the needy. This may have been the goal with socialist or communist local governments, although they have ultimately not proved to be all that popular! Generally, improvements in the education system have helped to take a toll of the more rigid and outdated aspects of Hinduism. However this has had side effects. One of the problems of modern education in poorer countries, if there are few jobs for graduates, is that it breeds an unemployed educated class which is cynical of the traditions and yet has no alternative means of finding life satisfaction. Religion does provide a reason for living for many in India, and millions obtain deep spiritual or mental benefits from practising their rituals and following their beliefs. The obvious, but incredibly difficult to attain, solution is to keep the best parts of Hindu culture and practice, and couple them with logical programmes for poverty and untouchability relief. One can read of incidents in India where untouchable castes have tried to enforce their lawful access to temples or wells, and for their troubles have been killed by other villagers.

After spending time in a number of small dwellings attached to little village temples, I still felt restless and undecided on the question of where to settle. My life had become a blur of places, people and events, and I was truly beginning to tire of wandering around India. I got to the stage where I decided to stop and stay where I was, which happened to be in a village some fifty miles east of Baroda. On the outskirts of a small village in some temple grounds I had found a dilapidated hut, which was adjacent to a tiny, hardly used temple. It would do for the time being, I thought although I did not know whether the local village would contain devotees who might look after my food needs. Staying in one spot, I realized, would be very different from traveling from place to place. Many Hindu villages would be happy to feed a sadhu who was just passing through. I did not like the idea of outstaying my welcome anywhere and did not know if the villages in this particular place would be keen on having a resident sadhu. Thus I was doubtful about staying in this particular area, but had decided to travel no further. Before moving into my new found dwelling, which was available to any passing sadhu who wished to use it, I decided to spend a few days as the guest of a very friendly goldsmith in a nearby village.

    That afternoon two men arrived to see me. They had traveled some ten miles by track, from an isolated village in an area inhabited mainly by farmers of a tribal caste. They had been sent as "envoys" to request me to come and stay in their village, which had on its outskirts a nice plot of temple land on a hill. There was a large "room" there built of mud and bricks, for the use of any sadhu who wished to stop off at the village. They said it was an ideal spot for me to stay and I would find the outlook and tranquility most congenial. They also told me that their village was the center for a dozen surrounding satellite hamlets, and it possessed a school, a dispensary, and rudimentary shops. It also had a daily bus service, (over dirt roads), to a main road, railway line, and a small town some seven miles away.

I discovered that the two men were emissaries for the group of upper caste Hindus who lived and worked in their village. This group was somewhat isolated amongst the non-vegetarian tribal castes who populated the area, and living in thatch huts and worshipped nature spirits rather than Hindu gods. The vegetarian, conscientious Hindus felt that their area was lacking in any traditional Hindu spiritual life, and hearing somehow of my search for a place to stay, had sent me an invitation to visit them. They were also promising to look after my basic food and other needs if I decided to reside in their village.

My goldsmith host and some of his neighbors had told me that the area to which I had been invited was inhabited by semi savage people who were only on the fringe of Hinduism. Most of them neither worshipped the Hindu gods, nor were interested in sadhus and holy men. My host tried to put me off going there. However, it felt to me that destiny was calling and I made arrangements to move to the village, which was called Kanod, later that week. As it was the rainy season and the bus to Kanod was often suspended due to flooded roads, I had to make sure first that the way by road would be feasible. Otherwise I would take the very muddy track route.

It turned out that when the same two men from Kanod, (both farmers of the Rajput or warrior caste), came to collect me on the chosen day the bus route was open. Although Kanod was ten miles by track, taking the bus meant a trip of thirty miles and changing buses three times. However, it was much easier this way than by going on foot and crossing the innumerable muddy gullies which had become streams in the wet season.

As we bumped along the gravel road in a dilapidated bus towards Kanod we were caught in a torrential downpour typical of the monsoon season. The skies opened up and soon we were crossing numerous streams that had sprung up instantaneously. At the approach to the village, the bus had to stop some two hundred yards short of its normal turning point just outside Kanod. A stream of some two to three feet in depth was rushing past, in what was normally a dry gully, and now formed a twenty-foot wide watery obstacle. Everyone got off the bus and merrily formed a human chain across the turgid waters, and I was helped over the flood this way to the crowd of villagers waiting on the other side.

It turned out that I had a large welcoming party waiting to receive, and garland me. Also present was a rather damp and bedraggled local band, of the village that was mostly used for wedding processions. I was ceremoniously paraded into the village to my temporary quarters. Just above the stream of water, on the village side, was a fifty foot bank and perched above it were the temple and the "house" I would be staying in.

Several people were working there in the rain at that very moment, putting in a cement floor and generally making the place habitable for me. For the present time I was to have a room in the village hall, and there I was to spend the next week nursing a heavy cold, while the skies poured torrents outside.

Kanod was in many respects a backwater, but there were friendly people keen to see that I became established at the little kutir*

* Kutir - hut like dwelling, of a sadhu.

To cook on I had one slow burning primus stove. Later I built a rough outdoor fireplace where I could cook rotis and chappaties over a wood fire and thus get the best flavor in my bread. Also I had a bed, mattress and mosquito net, although I found the area agreeably free of annoying insects.

Arrangements had been made for someone to come every morning to fetch pots of water from the nearest well some two hundred yards away down the hill, in order to give me sufficient for bathing, washing and cooking. For the equivalent of little more than a pound a month, a village girl would bring several head carried pots of water daily, as well as sweep inside and outside, and clean any dirty pots and pans. I was quite prepared to look after all my own needs, but one of the rules there was that women collect the water and do the cleaning. In my case, the village folk would have been embarrassed to see me carry my own water, and I was virtually forbidden to do so. Besides I would be taking away a job from the poorer village girls, who did a lot of housework for the wealthier households. Even an average household in India then, although incredibly poor by Western standards, could employ even poorer castes to do the cleaning, laundry and menial tasks. The richer families employ cooks, chauffeurs, night watchmen and so forth, although not usually on the scale of the British in the days of the Raj.

My role even as a poor sadhu was definitely "upper caste" as far as the village rules and rituals were concerned and any deviation on my part would have caused offence or embarrassment. I found that even with my small "income" of donated money, I was able regularly to employ some of the village urchins for help with my garden projects. Sometimes I would employ two boys all day, when they were not at school. I paid the standard rate for adult laborers at two rupees per eight-hour day. It was half a rupee more than the child's or woman's rate. At that time there were twenty rupees to the British pound: For many poor farmers in such villages as Kanod, supplementary paid laboring work is vital for their existence in the pre monsoon summer period. This covers the inevitable gap when their previous crop runs low or runs out altogether. Quite often I would find any work for the village boys to do in my garden, as I knew that just one rupee would buy a kilo of flour to feed their family that day. I was limited in the amount of work I could offer by my money supply, but when I received a larger sum I employed adults to do larger scale jobs like building proper steps up to the temple.

    Besides my room space, I had an outdoor verandah on one side, a tiny temple to look after, and an acre of land, including shady, bitter leaved medicinal neem trees. My plan was to develop the land into a garden with both shaded and flowery leisure areas and also to grow fruit trees and vegetables. Any villager could come and sit, away from the sparse, dry landscape, which was devoid of any eye pleasing shrubbery, due to the absence of irrigation and regular rain. Many village areas in India are sparse in terms of amenities such as gardens or parks, because in poorly watered places the population spends all their lives trying to survive by growing enough food in the monsoon and winter seasons. Villages with no irrigation can be very drab and dusty places for nine months of the year. If, however, there is any spare cash in the village, it may go towards building a temple or a communal garden space just in order to provide a little color or give a shady recreational area.

    I wished to make my little ashram into a well-watered haven for trees, shrubs and flowers, for all to enjoy. The trouble lay in getting water up to my area of land. I had to wait for two years until enough funds were collected to build a new well and to organize electricity and a pump. A lot of effort in the fund – raising for this enterprise was put in by one person, the village head man and doctor, who had been so instrumental initially in getting me to stay at Kanod. For two successive rainy seasons I planted a grove of trees only to see most of them wither away and die later due to the paucity of ground water from those two poor monsoons.

Many trees are planted each year in India by the forestry commissions, but if there is a poor monsoon, then a lot of their effort is wiped out. I got saplings free and often delivered, from local forestry offices, and tried hard to encourage tree planting all around the village by my own example. However, after a lot of work by my helpers, and me the results were saddening. Not a few saplings that survived the hot summer, succumbed to the ravages of hungry and persistent cows and goats in spite of thorn barriers.

I began to see why villagers did not bother too much with planting flowers or trees in their locality. It was too difficult to keep them protected, or the rainy seasons was too sparse, or too much rain fell and flooded or washed everything away. Outside the monsoon season, the sun was merciless for the rest of the year, especially in the furnace like, shimmering heat of summer days. Even winter days were hot when the sun was up and sunbathing was unwise.

During the two thirds of the year that I was at home in Kanod, I spent much of my day time in a state of inactivity, coming to life only in the cool of the mornings and evenings. The tin roof of my home produced unbearable heat during the hot days, so I had constructed a tile roofed open verandah with a raised platform on the side that faced the slight breezes. There I often sat and passed my time in a deck chair.

    Days, weeks, and months rushed by without really registering themselves. I had no need to clock anything or to regard time as having any influence on me. Christmas and birthdays did not exist for me, and only the big Hindu festivities brought some change into my routine. I was not bothered sitting in my deck chair or cross legged on a rug, about what was happening in the world or how my own life was passing by rapidly. I read no newspapers, I had no radio, or even time piece, and I was not interested in village gossip. I was quite content for long periods to let my *Prarabdha* take its course.

    Prarabdha is a Sanskrit term frequently seen in Vedanta texts. It means literally "the fruits of previous actions". A sannyasin is not supposed to do any activity (karma), which would create fresh Prarabdha to be experienced in the next or after life. The ultimate, (and proper), state for such a person is to let the fruits or consequences of previous actions. (in this or earlier lives), spend themselves naturally with the passage of time. According to Vedanta theory, Moksha or liberation from the cycle of birth and re-birth is obtained in this manner, i.e. when all Prarabdha is exhausted. Prarabdha is thus the passing of time and events that occur quite spontaneously without push or interference. To passively enjoy or suffer ones Prarabdha might seem to be an extremely negative attitude to life in terms of Western ideals and culture. In the West, the more one does or achieves, (especially materially), the more one is honored or respected. In Hindu philosophy the reverse can be true (In real life this can be sometimes true). In India the person who renounces worldly striving and accomplishments is often revered by many as a holy sage, a guru, and an altogether superior type of person.

Today in the West I believe that there is a somewhat undiscovered inclination towards the ideals of Vedanta philosophy, which promotes esoteric goals. Firstly many unemployed people, often by no choice of their own, have to come to terms with the prospect of time to spare - stretching out into the future. Secondly, people who have by self-effort obtained a large amount of leisure time for their own use, are growing in numbers. The leisure orientated lifestyle is becoming a fact of western life as further automation and affluence change roles and attitudes. At the moment, most people gear their leisure time to some form of physical activity where possible. However, the advancing increase of non-working hours could create more and more space for introspection and reflective mental activity.

My stay at Kanod was marked and dominated by the vast amount of leisure space that I had purely to myself. As there were not many diversions to keep me busy, I found that I could sit down to think about a subject, and continue my introspection in one direction for weeks on end. I did not become bored because I found even the most silent passage of time to be full of fascination. The day-to-day growth of a flower, or the scampering of a squirrel could hold my attention indefinitely. I sometimes thought that it would be interesting to be back in England, to use libraries, watch television and be entertained in numerous ways. When I did eventually return to England, I found that I quickly tired of the seemingly endless facilities for the occupation of leisure time. Much as children do with mud, sticks and stones, I gained more pleasure when I could occupy myself with the trivial but natural phenomena around me.

What was my mental level at that stage? Had I attained a state of self-knowledge and thus achieved Moksha? Furthermore, after all those years in India, had I found my own true religion and philosophy': If I had, did my beliefs prove to be lasting?

I developed a clearly defined philosophic outlook on life, which was not to change with the passage of time. I gained a deep mental satisfaction from my knowledge of Vedanta, and I find to this day that it guides me towards a calmness and equipoise, which alleviate the ups and downs of everyday life. My practice of yoga brought me to a stage where I had, if I wished, a strong degree of control over my life. For me, the sense of control over circumstances was, and is, mellowed by my acceptance by the doctrines of karma and Prarabdha, which means some surrender to the inevitability of fate.

My resignation to the whim of destiny did at times seem to make me a pessimist. However in the longer term I gained optimism and a belief that life's events are enacted by an ordained force, which works for our ultimate benefit. From this point of view the opposites of pain and pleasure, gain and loss, become equally acceptable. I had discovered that Mukti or Moksha is not a trance like state but simply the ability to accept the world as it is, and ourselves as we are. This does not preclude room for change, or personal endeavor, providing, that is, that one is able to be unaffected by success or failure. Also, that any objective or goal is itself not the only end. The journey, the effort, is also a goal. In terms of self-realization, what we seek to be or achieve is already within, already available.

The Self within, the Atman of the Vedanta, is so near and yet so hard to appreciate. All the Indian yogis and Gurus that I most respect, recommend the seeker to ash the Question, "Who am I?", and also to seek the guru within as well as without. Vedanta teachers say that when we ask ourselves, "Who am I?" we are trying to find out what the true nature of the "I" is. Not the mind, not the body, but an unchanging entity that remains constant in our waking, dream and sleep states. An entity, which remains constant through childhood, adolescence, adulthood and old age. It is the Self within, the Atman, which is the same "substance" as Brahma, the Cosmic Self.

*Brahma - a Sanskrit word for the impersonal "God". To be distinguished from Brahma, the Progenitor (one of the Vedic gods), and from a Brahmin, the highest caste.

    I cannot define precisely what my mental state was towards the end of my stay in India. This does not matter to me. I came to realize that the mind's activities are transient and fickle, whilst the light of yogic awareness burns steadily behind the mental screens. Once having reached the transcendental inner light or awareness through our deepest subconscious, we can return to our chosen life and continue on our way bathed in a subtle serenity. My quiet years in an isolated Gujerati village gave me the time and space to consolidate and fortify an inner awareness.

    During my stay at the small kutir in Kanod, I had few food supply problems. Often farmers would pass by my little temple after they had been out cutting by hand some crop or other. They would pop up and place a pile of wheat, rice, or pulse either in the temple or outside my door. This, plus regular donations of foodstuffs by other villagers and visitors, meant that I soon acquired stocks of grain. I had more than enough for myself and could feed any visiting sadhus or other guests. If I wished to cook, say, maize rotis, then I would fill a small tin box with maize grain and hand it, (with a small tip), to a village urchin for delivery to the local electric mill. In half an hour back would come the tin filled with freshly milled maize flour, warm and sweet smelling. Cooked over a wood fire and eaten hot such rotis of fresh flour would make a tasty meal, even on their own. A lot of the grain I used had been grown in fields fertilized by natural manure, (as the farmers could afford no other). Such grain produced much sweeter and tastier flour than the artificially fertilized version. In today's world of so -called "gourmet" foods, it is a pity that the real taste of naturally grown produce is experienced by few.

Almost daily during the cooler times of the day, I walked out into the surrounding area of field, scrub and gullies. During the season when crops were ripening, I would often be invited into someone's field to sample the produce. I had freshly picked corn on the cob roasted over twigs, or peanuts straight from the ground toasted in a similar fashion. Several farmers invited me to collect and pick green peas and pulses whenever needed for my pot. Vegetables were rarely grown by locals, even in the rainy season with the exception of chilies. Occasionally someone grew a few onions and perhaps potatoes or eggplants. Most villagers in this area, with the exception of the higher castes, rarely ate any vegetable dishes other than potatoes curried with fresh green or red chilies. In fact the average villager's vitamin intake seemed to be derived purely from the large quantities of hot peppers consumed, often ground up as a chutney. Frequently this was the only accompaniment to a roti meal in a poor household, where dhal and other "necessities" were unaffordable luxuries on many days of the year. I managed to grow a lot of vegetables in the rainy season, and planted peas, marrows and courgettes. In the summer I made use of lemons, which grew abundantly. Otherwise my vitamin intake was limited and irregular, especially as I could not eat chilies.

My body reacted to anything other than plain food, and in order to find out exactly how various foods affected me I experimented with a variety of diets. The diet that kept me in best health, I found, was a sparse regime of grains, pulses and vegetables - excluding salt, spices, sugar, tea, and all fatty products. I discovered that, perhaps due to the hot climate's effect and my lazy lifestyle, I could not happily digest oily food or milk products. At one time, for a month or so, I tried a diet of only fresh, hot rotis, with absolutely no other intake except water. This very plain regime of bread and water solely, did me no harm at all, and I even enjoyed the experience. In fact, I found that by having no variety of taste in my food, I was able (after a while) to derive just as much overall taste satisfaction from plain bread as from a varied diet.

I did not fully know then why I was so sensitive to so many food items. My weight since my arrival in India had been a very low 130 lbs., in spite of trying at previous times to put on pounds with rich foods. Also, I always ate large quantities of carbohydrates, even when I was on my simple diets. I feel that the large amounts of grain foods that I ate played a significant part in my skinniness, along with the debilitating effect of the intense heat. For slimmers I can recommend eating as much as you like providing you avoid sugar, processed white grain, and all fatty products. Whole wheat and pulse proteins help to produce a digestive fire within the body, akin to fueling a fire with dry twigs. Thus the appetite and the digestive powers are increased and .yet the body remains slim.

It is very difficult in India to avoid getting the occasional bout of a fairly serious illness. At Kanod I had a few alarming fevers. I hated taking antibiotics and during one bout of fever I became seriously ill and had an extremely high temperature. The village doctor persuaded me to take some Chloromycetin, and I duly recovered after a week or so. Afterwards I was told that probably I had suffered an attack of typhoid fever, and I could have died.

    There are all sorts of illnesses and hazards to be found in India, all waiting to kill one off very quickly. My destiny, however, was to come through, at least that period in India, unscathed. Villagers succumbed to illnesses like tetanus, usually after cutting themselves with a farm implement and then not seeking medical help. Rabies was another hazard. The towns and villages were full of mangy stray dogs, which were a health risk apart from their bites. Bites from another common creature, the snake, were an ever-present risk for the worker cutting crops by hand, especially as the time spent getting to the nearest medical help often meant certain death. A Kanod man got bitten on the head whilst carrying a bale of freshly cut grass. The snake had slithered into the bale somehow and bit the farmer as he was carrying it in the normal Indian fashion. He survived due to the immediate medical attention, and serum, he received at the Kanod dispensary.

I saw snakes around Kanod from time to time and some of them were huge. I glimpsed one sliding through the centre of a large bush. It was as thick as an arm and its body just kept sliding endlessly past. I never got to see its tail or head as I moved away pretty quickly. It was only on a few occasions that I saw any snakes around my kutir as I used to have a number of mongeese in nearby residence. I found a deadly poisonous snake in my room one day, but it left without much persuasion by prodding with a long stick. My main problem, especially in the monsoon season, was scorpions. They tended to scuttle around when the air was warm and humid, particularly at night. When I sat outside on such evenings or meditated in the dark, I always shone a torch around and looked carefully where I put my feet. Though not necessarily fatal, the scorpion sting gives a nasty jolt to the heart and produces much pain and swelling to follow. I once got stung on the finger by a baby one that was hidden in a, piece of moldy wood, which I had picked up for the fire. Its sting was like a large jolt of high voltage electricity shooting up my arm to my heart. Luckily little poison entered my finger, and I suffered briefly and mildly.

Scorpions carry their poisons in a little sac at the end of their tail. A needle like barb protrudes from the sac and is used for injecting the "victim". If I found a scorpion in my room, I would pick it up by the tail with the long tongs that I used for handling embers of the fire. Some kids from the village used to dig out scorpions from their holes in earth banks, and catch them by the tail with something suitable. Then they would cut off the poisonous sac, tie a string to the tail, and parade their newfound "pets" around for a while until the novelty wore off. I had a variety of animals dwelling in and around my acre plot. Squirrels nested between the walls and the roof of my kutir where there was quite a wide channel along the double thickness of the bricks. I could not see the channel but I could hear animals using it. Occasionally a baby squirrel would fall down from a hole in one corner into my room. The mother would then poke her head out and start squealing frantically while the baby stumbled around. The fall did not seem to do them any harm as even the smallest squirrel seems adept at landing upright and safe after a long drop. I used to grab the baby ones in a cloth and return them, squealing, to their home. I found out quite quickly that a thick cloth was necessary as even tiny squirrels have very sharp teeth. Rats were more unwelcome visitors and they also used the gap under the roof as a home at various times. They then scrambled down my walls at night to get at my food stores. I used to trap them and then release them a long way away in the fields. One other strange creature that took up residence was a giant armored lizard that looked like a small crocodile. I saw it once or twice in the evening on its way out to the fields. It was apparently a rare, shy creature that usually kept well away from human habitations. Less shy were the lizards that clung motionless to my inner wall during the day. They moved around at night and kept the place free of cockroaches. If they saw one they would pounce at great speed and gobble up their giant meal with a loud crunching noise.

    I was able to spend many hours observing the animals and birds around me, and also watch my flowers, saplings and plants grow (or wither) day by day. Nowadays I do not always notice the flora and fauna around me. It was only when I had endless time to sit and watch that I was really aware of nature's variety. In my home at Kanod the squirrels, the lizards, and even the rats were part of the animal family of my little temple area, and I was always aware of any changes in the wild life of my garden.

    In the very hot weather of summer, I took to sleeping outside where a mild breeze made the nights bearably cool. I had my bed above the ground of course, but I found that I slept very lightly, perhaps like an animal does, with some senses on guard. I felt that part of me was always awake, listening out for any untoward sounds. I can understand how an animal in the jungle feels, unable to relax like humans do in their secure houses.

    I was never too worried, however, about being on my own at night, in a corner of the fields without recourse to quick assistance in case of trouble. I had to accept and believe that the world around me was basically my nurturer and not my enemy. This attitude I have found to be of immense benefit, not just in "wild" places, but also in everyday life. After all, the modern world is itself a dense jungle, which harbors its own multitude of deadly perils, as well as being the provider of innumerable benefits.

Paramhansa Swami Ganeshi Giri
1975 Gujerat India

Paramhansa Swami Ganeshi Giri
(Procession held by villagers)
Moving into residence at Kanod village
1973 Gujerat India

CHAPTER TWELVE
Goodbye India

After nearly three years at Kanod I began to think that perhaps I was destined to spend the rest of my life in India. I thought deeply about making an effort to establish some sort of ashram or haven out of my humble surroundings. I wanted more than the simplicity around me and I hankered after developing the place into something, that was, frankly, materialistic in many respects. It took me a while to arrive at the very obvious, logical conclusion that I was not really happy with my simple Indian life, because I still aspired to the "affluence" that I knew I could have in England. After a while, I began to recognize again that my destiny was not, perhaps, after all the sadhu life, either spent in my little kutir or in wandering around India.

However I was traveling a lot to near and distant villages or towns to which I had been invited by a variety of "devotees". I gave a few talks or lectures here and there, and was starting to be the guru of a number of families spread over a wide area of Gujerat. I knew that if I was patient and built up my following over say ten years, then I could develop my base into an ashram that resembled something like that of my ambitions. However, quite suddenly the whole idea of staying in India started to seem rather strange and unnatural for me. In a most intriguing way I began to dream and think of England and. English things regularly. This was the re awakening, of an area of my mind that had seemed extinct. I started to think in English again, rather than in Hindi or the Gujerati in which I was becoming proficient. I began to appreciate speaking English when I met those who spoke it well, and started to seek out news of world events, and to read books on non-religious subjects. I began even to think of my parents for the first time in eight or nine years. I had a peculiar feeling as if a veil had suddenly been lifted, allowing my previous identity as Raymond to intermingle with my Indian role as Ganesh Giri. I sensed that my life in India was reaching the point of maturity, and that I could achieve no more in my endeavors to fathom the depths of Hinduism and yogic lore. I did not feel that I had achieved the perfection of my sadhu lifestyle, but then I no longer needed such a goal. Something was pulling me in a radical new direction, not for the first time in my life.

My thoughts went back to earlier days and the causes of my trip to India.

The roots of my physical and mental journey East had originated in the early nineteen sixties when I was a pupil at grammar school. For society in Britain, that era was part of a special time of change. The new trends in music played a major role during that period, because the sounds and lifestyles of people like the Beatles and Rolling Stones enormously influenced the adolescents who had been born in the post War baby boom. The sixties was a revolutionary time for the values and activities of the young, and brought about a deep upheaval of social attitudes.

At the age of fifteen, I was living on a council estate in London, where most teenagers became either "Mods or Rockers".

Mods were smart, fashionable dressers who rode motor scooters; Rockers wore leather gear and rode motor bikes.

I took to hanging around with the Mods at local dance halls where bands such as the Yardbirds used to play. When I left school at sixteen, I had become interested in rhythm and blues music and began to visit pubs where this music was played and long haired hippies congregated. In those days, hippies were better known as Beatniks or Beats. The Mods were beginning to use drugs such as "speed" "purple hearts", which helped them to stay awake in the all night music clubs. `The hippy fraternity favored the use of hashish or "hash". The exponents of the drop out lifestyle were already roaming abroad to Istanbul for the cheap living and cheap drugs. Later, many thousands would make the overland trip to Kabul and Katmandu; (which became a mecca for hippy pilgrims.)

I was unhappy with my life in England and felt restless. As a child even, I had been intrigued by stories of wanderers and travelers who lived in primitive conditions. I considered myself over restricted at home and wanted to live a free and simple life with the minimum of possessions and comforts, and to pay little heed to the norms of society. The books I had read at an earlier age had influenced me deeply. They had been about explorers in the Amazon or hunters of man eating tigers in India. In those days I often dreamt that I was sleeping rough under the stars, cooking over a wood fire, or paddling down a jungle river. Sometimes at night I felt unhappy, cosseted in my warm bed knowing that all my food and clothing needs were met. Sometimes I got out of bed and slept on the floor with only one blanket. I think that the desire to be an explorer and traveler was really deeply ingrained within me, and it was this that eventually took me such a long way from home and into years of adventure.

My first rebellion from society began with my leaving home with a sleeping bag and joining the hippies. I spent a few weeks sleeping under piers, in derelict houses, and by the river Thames before I returned home. My parents were very upset by my behavior, especially as they had struggled to see me through grammar school, and by the fact that I had given up my first job as a scientific assistant. I found another job as a casual laborer, but planned to leave home for good. I decided to travel the world, with Istanbul as my first objective. My parents seemed to feel that by going overseas I would get whatever ailed me out of my system. Certainly, at home I was morose, uncooperative and uncommunicative.

In my new, strange mood in Kanod I felt the desire to communicate with my parents and wrote a letter saying, "Sorry I haven't written for nine years, but I've been a Hindu monk". The reply from England expressed surprised relief, they had thought I was dead. Would I return? An airplane ticket would be sent to me immediately if I so desired. As easy as that, I thought, just hop on a plane and become a different person. I had no doubt then that I would not remain the Hindu Ganesh Giri once I left India.

I did not want to disappoint the Indian people around me, nor the India that had mothered and nurtured me all those years. I felt that I would be letting down everyone and everything that I had lived for if I turned round and said, "Well, this Hindu religion business is all right, but I've got new plans now". I was quite shocked by my sudden change of heart and mind, although I knew that just as I had been pulled by a magnet to India, now the magnet had reversed its current and was drawing me back to England. I also realized that the experience to come would make me wiser and would not destroy all the good things I had learnt in India.

Despite feeling anguish over leaving my developing guru role and disappointing my Indian "devotees", I said yes to the air ticket home. I said my goodbyes to a somewhat bewildered number of Kanod villagers, and to other followers and helpers. I set off once more to Bombay, this time to leave from the city in which I had arrived some ten years before. I found that before I could collect my ticket, I had to have police and income tax clearance, involving visiting a number of offices. The officials were surprised to see that I had spent ten years in India and was declaring zero earned income. However, the highest official that I had to see was a disciple of Swami. Muktananda and when he learnt of my stay at the Ganesh Puri ashram, he was most helpful. In fact my visits to the various offices consisted mainly of having friendly chats over cups of tea, without hardly mentioning my formal business.

Departure day arrived and I set off (on my first air trip) for London by Egypt Air. I was wearing a new pair of thick, homespun dhotis and a shawl. I spent my last days in Bombay staying with the doctor brother of Kanod's head man. A friend of his saw me off on my 1 am flight and gave me some money. I had then the grand sum of one hundred rupees, (about five pounds), to spend on my arrival in London. I arrived at Heathrow, nearly eleven years after leaving England, somewhat bewildered and took a taxi home to mum and dad. Surprisingly the homecoming was not a shock, but quite a, subdued affair. I felt almost as if I had been away on a package tour for a couple of weeks!

Within a few days I felt that I had lived in England all my life and also discovered that I now got on very well with my parents. I quickly took to wearing shirts, trousers, socks and shoes, and after two weeks I hardly felt that I had been a Hindu sadhu for ten years.

I went to look for a job and soon had a temporary post as in the laundry room of the hospital where my father worked. I found work to be no problem at all, just boring after a while in that particular case. Soon I was accepted to do three years training as a student psychiatric nurse and moved to live in nurses' quarters. It was a new phase of my life that was to prove very interesting.

After qualifying I moved to New Zealand and began a further series of travels and adventures. Wherever I went, however, I took with me the simple philosophy that I had gained from my years in India, What I had been looking for was already part of me - if not all of me.

THE END.

About Raymond

In my younger years I was a monk in India for 10 years.

Hence I write & talk about Yoga, Mantras, Kundalini, and Gurus.

Titles include: *Om Divine Grace / Goddess Inspired - collected writings / Divine Grace Journey.*

Om Divine Grace Podcasts.

mantra guru raymond YouTube for kundalini tutorials.

www.VSUAL.com for Mantra Art – my artistic endeavours.

I have been a Mental Health Practitioner since 1980.

My Spiritual Practice & use of Mantras has helped to lead me towards mental, physical & spiritual health.

Get a Mantra for Enlightenment!

www.goddessmantra.guru

I have a Multi-faith perspective regarding my religious beliefs. I am focused on what has worked for me, & am now not affiliated to any path, group, or movement, (except my own!). However I do believe that Divine Grace has got me where I am, & now guides me. (And illuminates me about the yoga, mantras & devotions that I use)

I seek to share my experience & knowledge as a service to others, whilst respecting totally others beliefs, & what may work best for you.

English Man, Beggar Man, Holy Man.   Raymond Pattison

www.ingramcontent.com/pod-product-compliance
Lightning Source LLC
Chambersburg PA
CBHW051422290426
44109CB00016B/1396